DEADLY DADS

OF THE

UK

PATERNAL FILICIDE

SYLVIA PERRINI

PUBLISHED BY:

GOLDMINEGUIDES.COM

Copyright © 2013

Sylviaperrini.goldmineguides.com

All rights reserved.

No part of this publication may be copied, reproduced in any format, by any means, electronic or otherwise, without prior consent from the copyright owner and publisher of this book.

This book is for informational and entertainment purposes. The author or the publisher will not be held responsible for the use of any information contained within this eBook.

DISCLAIMER

In researching this book, I gathered material from a wide variety of resources, newspapers, academic papers, and other material both on and offline. In many cases, I have referenced actual quotes pertaining to the content throughout. To the best of my knowledge, the material contained is correct. Neither the publisher nor the author will be held liable for incorrect or factual mistakes.

TABLE OF CONTENTS

INTRODUCTION	1
SUKHDEV SANDHU	5
WAYNE SKERTON	17
STEPHEN CARTER	19
PETER STAFFORD	20
ZAINULABEDIN ZAIDI	23
PHILLIP AUSTIN	30
ROBERT MOCHRIE	38
FRANK FAIRLESS	50
KARL BLUESTONE	52

STEVEN WILSON	59
KEITH YOUNG	75
JAYA PRAKASH CHITI	82
RICHARD HICKS	91
GAVIN HALL	101
ROBERT THOMSON	107
ASHOK KALYANJEE	111
BRIAN PHILCOX	120
CHRIS FOSTER	126
DAVID CASS	152
HUGH MCFALL	156

WAYNE ACOTT	**160**
ARAM AZIZ	**171**
CERI FULLER	**173**
GRAHAM ANDERSON	**198**
MICHAEL PEDERSON	**200**
JULIAN STEVENSON	**215**
CONCLUSION	**218**

INTRODUCTION

As an author, I am far better known for writing about women murderers than men. However, after having stumbled across the shocking story of John List, an American man who annihilated his mother, wife, and three teenage children and then managed to evade capture for over 18 years and when finally apprehended never expressed remorse for his crimes, I began to wonder if similar crimes had been committed in the United Kingdom.

My research shocked me. I was completely horrified at the statistics I found.

EVERY TEN DAYS IN ENGLAND AND WALES ONE CHILD IS KILLED AT THE HANDS OF HIS OR HER PARENT. IN OVER TWO THIRDS (67% ON AVERAGE) OF ALL

CASES OF CHILDREN KILLED AT THE HANDS OF ANOTHER PERSON, THE PARENT IS THE PRINCIPAL SUSPECT (FROM: OFFICE FOR NATIONAL STATISTICS (2013) FOCUS ON: VIOLENT CRIME AND SEXUAL OFFENCES, 2011/12. [NEWPORT]: OFFICE FOR NATIONAL STATISTICS (ONS))

And even more chilling is that it is estimated that murders in which a father kills his children, and sometimes his partner, and then frequently themselves, occurs about every six to eight weeks in the United Kingdom.

Of all the hideous violent crimes that are committed, the murder of one's own children, one's own flesh and blood, are the most baffling. The majority of parents, thank goodness, would do anything to protect their children and would even die to save their children. So for a parent to look at his or her child, perhaps hear their pleas and cries, and watch their uncomprehending faces, and murder them, is almost too heinous to think about. We immediately presume

INTRODUCTION

the parent must have lost his or her mind in a temporary moment of insanity or madness. It is hardly surprising that we find ourselves recoiling in horror at such appalling tragedies and comfort ourselves by thinking that they are isolated, senseless, incidents.

Statistics show that a child in the United Kingdom is far more likely to be murdered by a parent than by a stranger. Even more horrifying is that many of the murders committed by fathers, as in the John List case in the United States, are premeditated.

What can possibly make a father commit such unspeakable savagery against his family? Is it despair, hatred, or revenge, or a hideous, deranged possessive love or an incomprehensible abnormality? Are these fathers normal men driven to the edge when circumstances in their lives go wrong or just devilish fiends? As of this time, December 2013, it is an immensely under-researched area.

Unfortunately, as demonstrated in the following profiles in this book, and there are a great many more than those I have included, these kinds of murders are not as rare as we would like to believe.

SUKHDEV SANDHU

Sarah Heatley was one of four daughters in a close loving family. She grew up in the Midlands. In her early 20s, she took a job as a nurse at Queen Mary's Hospital Roehampton in West London. In 1987, at the age of 23, Sarah met Sukhdev Sandhu who was a 28-year-old, 6ft tall, 210lbs, westernized Indian Sikh. He was, at the time, the junior doctor on her ward and was known by the Anglicized name of Dave. He was intelligent, attractive, and swept her off her feet.

When, after an eight month relationship, Dave was offered a job in Sheffield Hospital in Northern England, Sarah joined him. They married in October of 1988 and had two children in quick succession, Nina on March 12, 1989 and Jack on April 17, 1990.

DEADLY DADS OF THE UK

In 1992, Dave opened his own practice as a General Practioner, a long held dream of his. Sarah, with the children in nursery school, returned to work at the hospital in Sheffield. They appeared the perfect, young, successful family, living in a four-bedroomed house set on an acre of gardens, with nice expensive cars. They appeared to have achieved the middle class dream. Then, slowly, Sarah's dream life began to fall apart. Unknown to Sarah, they were living way beyond their means. As Dave became increasingly in debt, he began to become increasingly controlling and violent physically and verbally towards Sarah.

He allowed her a small allowance for lunch and to get her to work and back. And although the bank account was in both their names, Dave had all the bank cards. At the time, Sarah, still deeply in love with her husband, put it all down to stress and thought it was simply a blip in their marriage that would pass. Within a short amount of time, he controlled her financially and emotionally.

One night, in May of 1993, Sarah had gone to

bed early. Dave was out, and her son Jack had crawled into bed with her. She was woken by her husband, who had been drinking. He knelt on her chest and began battering her about the face. Their son Jack woke up and began screaming,

"Don't hit my mommy! Don't hit my mommy!"

Dave removed Jack from the room before returning where he continued bashing Sarah with his fists until her eyes were black and her nose bled. Throughout the beating, he shouted obscenities at her and threatened to kill her. The following morning, unlike some male abusers, he showed no sign of remorse.

For the next three months, Sarah did exactly what her husband told her to do. She went to bed when he said, got up when he said, and went to the supermarket only with his consent. If he demanded a cup of tea, he got it. If he felt annoyed by her, he would call her a bad mother, a whore, or a lousy lover. Sometimes, he would threaten to break her legs if she went near the children. Sarah was terrified by the hate directed towards her.

For Sarah, the last straw occurred three months later in August. Dave became furious with her because she hadn't remembered to place fresh food in the cat's bowl. He threatened to kill her. He said,

"I should have killed you last time. I'll do it properly next time."

Sarah finally confided in her twin sister Ruth, who persuaded her to tell her parents the situation. Sarah took Ruth's advice.

On August 15, Sarah's parents arrived at the family home accompanied by police officers to escort Sarah and the children out of the family home. As they were leaving the house, Dave appeared in the hallway and asked,

"Where are you going?"

Sarah replied simply by saying, "I'm leaving."

With the police in attendance, there was little

Dave could do.

However, within three days after Sarah left the family home, Dave turned up at her parents' house in Chesterfield, yelling, threatening, and pleading.

She refused to see him, which didn't prevent him from bombarding her with hate letters and phone calls.

On August 28, Sarah succeeded in gaining a restraining order to make Dave stay away. The order was granted on condition that she start divorce proceedings. This only enraged Dave all the more.

With the restraining order in place, Sarah, after three weeks at her parents' house, got a hospital workers apartment in Sheffield and returned to work. Meanwhile, a court welfare officer was given ten weeks to assess their case.

Dave's mental state was becoming increasingly bizarre. In October of 1993, he was signed off work and taken to a psychiatric unit after begging a friend to kill him. By the time the psychiatrist saw him, he was lucid again and was sent home.

Over the months of separation before their court case about custody of the children was heard, Dave would taunt Sarah by saying,

"You'll never keep them from me. I will take them somewhere where you will never see them again."

At that point, she wasn't worried Dave would hurt the children because she believed he loved them, but she was worried about him abducting them and possibly taking them to India. For this reason, she asked the court not to allow Dave unsupervised access to the children.

On December 10, 1993, Dave and Sarah attended the family court. Dave was dressed immaculately in a business suit and looked the perfect, respectable, and responsible family doctor; an upstanding member of the community.

The welfare officer who had been assigned to their case described Sarah as 'intransigent' and suggested that she was "making her husband's emotional state even worse" and was "determined to exaggerate the fear of him abducting the children."

The officer acknowledged that Dave had, at one point, been suicidal but said in his opinion, "he now seemed better." Dave certainly presented to the court the image of a stable, affable, generous, intelligent, and, loving father.

After about three hours of legal arguments, Sarah's lawyer advised her to agree to her husband's demand for unsupervised access to the children. He said that if she continued to object she and Dave would be called to the witness stand, where they would end up carrying out character assassinations of each other and at the end of that, the judge would grant him time alone with the children anyway and weekend access, no matter how badly Dave had beaten her. He said she would never convince the court that her husband was mentally unstable. Sarah argued vehemently with her attorney against Dave being allowed unsupervised access to their children but eventually caved in.

The court ordered three hour weekly unsupervised contact times and two overnight weekend visits per month.

It was during the three hourly week times that Sarah began to not only fear her estranged husband might abduct the children but might also harm them. Dave, to provoke Sarah, would tell the children they needn't wear their car seatbelts, which he knew would worry her. She began to realize that his hatred of her was greater than his love for their children; a truly shattering and deeply disturbing revelation.

On Saturday February 5, 1994, Jack and Nina had their first unsupervised weekend with their father; Sarah nervously kissed her children goodbye. Dave was to return the children to Sarah late the following afternoon.

At 2.30 p.m. on the chilly Sunday afternoon of February 6, 1994, Sarah was in her kitchen preparing the children's tea, when her doorbell rang. Thinking and hoping it may have been Dave returning the children early, she rushed to open it. Her face dropped at the sight of two sombre faced policemen. Her first thought was that Dave had abducted them.

One police officer simply said,

"There's no easy way to say this. Your husband has killed your children.

****

Jack & Nina

Nina, age four, and Jack, age three, had been found at Dave's Sheffield home, strangled by a pajama belt. The post-mortem thought that at the time of their deaths on Sunday morning, the children had been awake and given that he couldn't have killed them at the same time, one supposed that one child was probably aware of what was coming. After strangling them, Dave wrapped their bodies in duvets and took them to the cellar of the house and left them.

The police discovered Dave's body some hours later at the foot of a block of apartments, from which he had thrown himself.

In his house, the police discovered a videotape Dave had made of the children the day before. In the tape, he was asking whether they wanted to 'stay with daddy' and whether they agreed that 'mommy was bad'.

The police advised Sarah not to watch it. She heeded their advice. She believes he left it for some kind of justification for his actions.

For their funeral, Sarah dressed Nina in a white party dress and Jack in his beloved fireman's outfit. They were buried together, their fingers entwined in a single white coffin.

In an emotional interview shortly after the murders, Sarah was reported as saying:

"How I wished Dave had killed me. Killing the children and leaving me alive was the worst possible thing he could do."

After the murders of her children, Sarah moved back in with her parents but with nightmares of the last moments of Jack and Nina haunting her, she moved to Greece for a while and took a job in a bar in an attempt to drown the memories. Then finding her life empty and pointless, she moved back to Sheffield and resumed nursing. Eventually, she entered into a relationship with a divorced university lecturer and out of the relationship, her son George was born. The relationship didn't last, but she and George's father remain good friends.

Sarah firmly believes that she let Nina and Jack down by not challenging the decision to allow her husband to have unsupervised visits.

Sarah Heatley now campaigns tirelessly for changes to the legal system to prioritize protection for children's safety. She has taken part in many television documentaries, held talks with the Lord Chancellor's office, and works with the NSPCC and Women's Aid, the UK charity that specializes in domestic violence.

Speaking of Dave, Nina, and Jack Sarah says:

"All of them were betrayed by a flawed legal system that enabled my husband to kill Nina and Jack by placing them in his care."

Sarah firmly believes that her children's murders could have been prevented.

WAYNE SKERTON

On March 23, 1994, Wayne Skerton, from Plymouth, broke up with his wife, who was his childhood sweetheart. He then drove his two young sons Joshua, 2, and Sam, 4, to a beautiful spot in Dartmoor, Devon. Here, he parked the car and inserted a hose into the exhaust of his Ford Sierra and fed it into the interior of his car. Climbing back into his car, he held Joshua on his lap while Sam played with his toys on the backseat. The car overheated and the engine stalled.

They were found and rushed to hospital. Wayne and Sam survived, but Joshua suffered brain damage and died a few days later.

At his trial on November 21st, 1994 at Plymouth

Crown Court, Wayne pled guilty to the manslaughter of his two-year-old son Joshua and grievous bodily harm to his four-year-old son Sam.

Wayne Skerton was jailed for four years for manslaughter due to mental incapacity.

STEPHEN CARTER

In April of 1999, Stephen Carter, a factory manager from Weaver Hills, Staffordshire, killed his three children following the break-up of his marriage and then committed suicide.

At the inquest into the murders, the coroner, John Wain, said:

"Carter wanted to destroy everything he held of great value in his life. Regrettably, this included his own children."

PETER STAFFORD

On Monday afternoon, October 4, 1999, police broke into a terraced house in Sparkhill, Birmingham, after the children's grandfather had become concerned at not hearing or receiving any answer to his knocking on the door of the Stafford family.

Inspector Phil Wright, of the West Midlands Police, described the crime scene they encountered in the house as the most horrific he had seen in over 20 years' of service.

On entering the house, they found Helen Stafford, 30, and her three children Kellie, 7, Daniel, 6, and Joe, 2, all stabbed to death. Helen also had wounds to her head.

PETER STAFFORD

The father, Peter Stafford, who police established had stabbed his children and wife, was found hanging from the stair banister of the house.

Neighbors were in total shock as the couple had appeared as a completely normal, happily devoted family who cared about each other.

Kellie, 7, Daniel, 6, and Joe, 2,

Peter and Helen had run and operated their own cleaning business together. The dreadful massacre was blamed on financial worries and depression suffered by Peter Stafford.

Relatives of the deceased family decided they should all be buried together. A funeral service was held at St James the Great Church in Shirley, near Birmingham in October of 1999.

The Reverend Peter Babington told attending mourners not to look for an explanation for what had happened or to seek to blame anyone for the killings.

"None of us can really imagine what leads anyone to take the lives of their family and themselves," he said.

"Many people are, I know, feeling a deep anger about what happened but in this I think we must take our lead from the immediate family, whose wishes from the first have been that Helen, Pete, Kellie, Dan, and Joe should be together now."

The five coffins, all topped with flowers, were taken away from the church in three hearses for cremation.

ZAINULABEDIN ZAIDI

On March 17, 2000, an English emergency operator received a chilling call from a young child that was taped.

Operator: "Emergency Services."

Child: "Hello, can I get that. Can I have the police please?"

Operator: "We are the police, thank you."

Child: "Oh (in the background noisy breathing and faint screaming could be heard) Can I? Can I?"

Operator: "If you can bear with me… if you stay on the line, I'm connecting you now."

Controller: "Wants the police. Not ringing. (Noisy breathing heard in the background)

Operator: "Yeah, if you can stay on the line I will be as quick as I can."

Child: "Quickly, because my dad, erm, is getting my mom and stabbing and killing her."

Operator: "Yeah, I'll be as quick as I can for you now." (In the background screaming; bleeping tones; scream.)

Operator: "Hello. You're through to the Emergency Services. Is anyone there?"

Child: "Don't kill me, Daddy."

At this point the line went dead.

Zainulabedin Zaidi was a strict Muslim banker. In an arranged marriage in England in 1988, he married Shazia Rathore, a social worker. They had two children together, a daughter, Saba and a son, Zeshan.

Shazia, who had had a far more westernized upbringing than Zainulabedin, was deeply unhappy in her marriage as she found her husband far too possessive and restrictive of her movements. He would not allow her to leave the house by herself, nor even allow her to visit her doctor alone.

In 1997, after nine unhappy years, she had had enough and left the marriage and family home in Goodman Park, Slough, Berkshire, with the children and filed for divorce. She moved to Bracknell about twenty miles from Slough, to be nearer her parents and twin sister. Here, she got a job at Wexham Park Hospital in Slough as a social worker.

The divorce courts granted Zainulabedin weekend custody rights to his children. When he went to pick the children up on Friday afternoons, he forbade his former wife from looking or speaking to him.

In 1999, Shazia remarried, a fact that she attempted unsuccessfully to keep hidden from her jealous ex-husband.

On the Friday afternoon of the 17th of March 2000, Zainulabedin, 34, arrived at Shazia's house at 3.30 p.m. which was the normal time he called to pick up his children for the weekend. As was customary when he was at the house, Shazia's new husband, Saeed Dogar, made himself scarce. On this occasion, he went to a butcher's shop to buy meat for an evening meal to celebrate the Muslim festival of *Eid-ul-Adha*.

When Shazia, 27, opened the front door to her ex-husband, he pushed her violently into the house and shut and bolted the door behind him. In front of his two terrified children Saba, 7, and Zeeshan, 6, he pulled out a knife with a seven-inch blade and began frenziedly stabbing Shazia in her face. She suffered deep cuts to her hands as she put her hands out to defend herself as blood splattered the hall walls. Crawling into the living room, Zainulabedin followed her as the children bolted upstairs to the main bedroom, and Zeeshan made the frantic call to Emergency Services.

Sahia suffered stab wounds, some as deep as 20cm, to her face, hands, and chest before Zainulabedin slit her throat. Leaving his ex-wife dead on the blood soaked living room carpet, Zainulabedin made his way upstairs to attend to his children. Both children died from stab wounds to their neck and throat. Their bodies were found lying a few feet apart from each other. The child that was last to be murdered must have witnessed not only the killing of their mother but also of their sibling.

When Zainulabedin had finished his grisly task, he made his way back downstairs and placed the knife in a bowl under the sink. He later disposed of his blood-spattered clothing and cleaned himself up, before going to an Indian restaurant for a curry.

Saeed Dogar arrived back at the house from his grocery shopping and discovered the horrific massacre of his wife and step-children.

The police put out a nationwide appeal for information as to the whereabouts of Zainulabedin Zaidi. He was arrested the following day in High Wycombe, Buckinghamshire. He was charged with the murders of his ex-wife Shazia, his daughter Saba, and son Zeeshan. In his initial questioning, he tried to put the blame for the deaths on Shazia's new husband.

Shazia, Saba, and Zeeshan.

At his trial, despite overwhelming forensic evidence and the taped telephone conversation by his six-year-old son to the Emergency Services, he denied any involvement in the death of his family and refused to give evidence.

A jury of eight men and four women took just two and a half hours to convict him of three counts of murder after an eight-day trial at Reading Crown Court in the autumn of 2000.

The judge, Mr. Justice Moises, before sentencing Zainulabedin said to him,

"Once in the house, you stabbed and cut Shazia's throat. You then stabbed and cut the throats of both your son and daughter. They knew what you were about to do. One of them pleaded with you not to kill them."

He then sentenced him to three life sentences and told him that he must serve twenty years before parole is even considered.

Zainulabedin Zaidi has never shown any remorse for the murders.

PHILLIP AUSTIN

Carol Quinn was feeling unsettled. She had been trying to get a hold of her daughter Claire for a week despite leaving countless messages on her home and mobile phones. The last time she had seen her daughter was on Thursday July 6, 2000 when they had enjoyed a shopping trip and lunch together. Claire and her husband Philip and their two children, Keiren and Jade, had recently returned from a family holiday in the Canary Isles in Spain, and Claire appeared happy and was excitedly talking about maybe booking another holiday.

Normally, the mother and daughter, who had a close relationship, spoke on the telephone every day and sometimes several times a day. The last time she had spoken to Claire was on the afternoon of Sunday, July 9. Later that evening, Carol had phoned Claire again and her husband, Phillip, had answered the phone. To Carol, he sounded quiet and cold and told her that Claire wasn't there. Carol assumed the couple must have had a fight; not unheard of and normally concerning money or the lack of.

Claire and Philip had met in Northampton in 1990. They soon became a couple and moved in together. Philip worked as a warehouse forklift driver, and Claire worked for Northamptonshire County Council as an auxiliary nurse.

The pair worked hard and within 18 months had saved enough to buy, with a mortgage, a three-bedroom Victorian terrace house in Stockmead Road Northampton. That same year, 1992, Claire had given birth to a baby boy, Keiren, followed not long after by a baby girl, Jade, born in April of 1993. Philip and Claire married in July of 1993.

Like many young couples with mortgage repayments and the financial costs of two young children, the couple struggled. Claire returned to work part time, and Philip began working the night shifts that paid more. He also worked overtime as much as possible to boost the family income. Sometimes, in the day time when Claire was at work, he would, rather than sleep, have to care for the children causing him to become irritable and shout at the children, which would then cause rows between him and Claire.

Sometimes, after the rows, he would disappear for a few days, causing Claire to give him the nickname 'Gulliver.'

As Carol fretted over why her daughter wasn't returning her calls, her home phone rang on the afternoon of Monday, July 17, 2000. It was the secretary from her grandchildren's school, Standens Barn Lower School. She said she'd had a phone call from neighbors of Jade and Keiren who were concerned at not having seen the children and that Jade and Keiren hadn't been at school, nor had she been able to get hold of either of their parents. Carol immediately knew something was wrong. Very wrong.

Carol phoned her husband, Harry Quinn, 62, Claire's stepfather, at work at the flour-mill where he was chief engineer. He, reacting to the urgency in her voice, immediately left work and drove to their home in Bugbrooke, Northamptonshire. He picked Carol up before driving the 12 miles to Claire's spacious house.

It was a warm summer's afternoon on July 17, 2000 when Harry pulled up outside Claire's house. His face was tense. Carol's stomach was doing somersaults. She didn't know what to expect, but it certainly wasn't the scene she found; a scene for which nothing could have prepared her.

Carol and Harry let themselves into Claire's family home, and a horrible smell pervaded their senses. Lying on the blood-soaked floor of the kitchen was her 31-year-old daughter Claire, who had been stabbed to death with such savage force that the knife used to attack her had snapped. Beside her lay Dandy and Sooty, the family's pet poodles, who had been beaten to death with a mallet. Blood splattered the walls and furniture. In complete terror, Carol ran up the stairs of the three-bedroom house, hoping and praying to find her two grandchildren safe. Bursting into eight-year-old Keiran's room, she found his lifeless body lying face down on his bed. A teddy bear sat on his pillow. Feeling as if she was in a horror movie, she stumbled into seven-year-old Jade's room to discover her lying dead on her bedroom floor, with the belt from her pink dressing gown tied around her neck.

Distraught and hysterical, Carol and Harry ran next door to a neighbor's house and phoned the police. That night, at Kettering General Hospital, Carol and Harry formally identified the bodies.

The police, upon arriving at the scene and assessing the evidence, immediately put out a nationwide search for Phillip Austin. He had been absent from work for about a week and was known to drive a blue Pruton car. Police believed the murders had happened a week prior to the bodies being discovered and found that Philip had taken out a £5,000 loan shortly before the murders had been committed.

Neighbors of the family were all shocked as they all expressed the view that,

"They seemed to be a quiet, normal family."

It was not too long before the police located Philip and arrested him for the murders of his wife and two children.

Phillip, at first, pleaded not guilty to the murders on the grounds of diminished responsibility but at his trial at Northampton Crown Court, on March 22, 2001, he changed his plea to guilty.

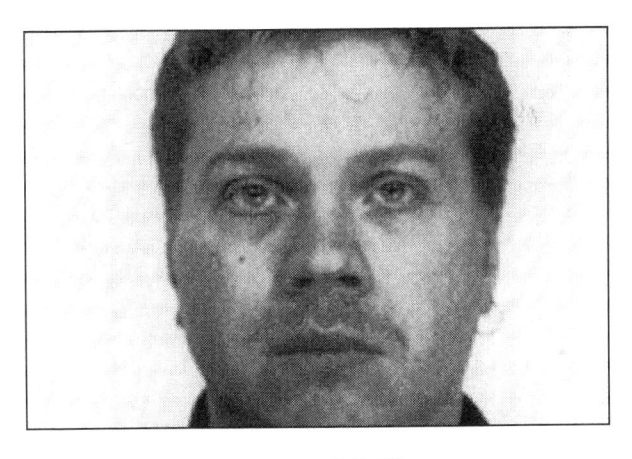

PHILIP AUSTIN

The court heard from the prosecution, backed up by forensic evidence, that there had been a desperate struggle between the couple in the hallway. Here, Phillip had hit Claire over the head with a mallet before dragging his wife into the kitchen, where he repeatedly stabbed her with two carving knives with such savagery that one of the knives broke. He had then pounded the skulls of Dandy and Sooty, two pet poodles, with the mallet.

Philip then calmly informed Claire's boss that she had injured her back whilst moving furniture and would be off work for a few days. He then went and removed his blood stained clothes, showered, and dressed in clean clothes before leaving the house to pick his children up from school.

On the way home from school, he took them for fish and chips and doped them with herbal sleeping tablets. He drove them around aimlessly until they had both fallen asleep on the back seat of his car before taking them home and carrying them both up to their respective bedrooms.

He strangled Keiren with a pair of toddler suspenders and Jade with a dressing gown belt. The children were so tired they put up little resistance.

Philip then fled the house taking with him the £5,000.

The prosecutors said that when Philip was asked by the police why he had murdered Claire he said,

"She started hassling me and arguing and that I just turned on her."

When asked why he had then killed the children, he replied,

"It sort of came to me that I had killed her so I killed my children."

Philip Austin was sentenced to three life sentences.

ROBERT MOCHRIE

On the night of July 12, 2000, on what had been a beautiful summers day, Robert Mochrie, 49, bludgeoned to death his wife Catherine, 45, his daughters Sian, 16, and Bethan, 10, and his sons James, 18, and Luke, 14, and then hanged himself. He left behind no note and no clue as to his motivation for slaughtering his own flesh and blood.

Neighbors and friends were totally shocked and horrified as the family appeared to be a perfectly normal and happy suburban Catholic Church going family.

Robert and Catherine had married in 1977 when he was a civil servant. Throughout their 23-year marriage, each had held traditional roles: Robert was the financial person and breadwinner, and Catherine the home-maker.

In 1985, they bought a large five bedroomed family home in a cul-de-sac, 43 Rutland Close on the Highlight Estate on the outskirts of Barry, a seaside resort less than 7 miles south of the capital city of Wales, Cardiff. Largely young professionals populated the Highlight Estate with the houses having brick-paved driveways, neatly cut lawns, and patios.

In 1990, Robert was referred to a psychiatrist, Dr. Brian Harris, with depression. He told Dr. Harris that he felt suicidal and that problems at his work place made him feel as if "someone had blown his head open with a shotgun." He refused to be admitted to a psychiatric unit or for his wife to to be informed about his condition. He was prescribed anti-depressants and his condition improved.

Robert was referred again to Dr. Harris in November of 1993 with depression and was again prescribed anti-depressants. Around about this time, his youngest son Luke, at the age of eight, was diagnosed with a life-threatening brain tumor that left him with minor learning difficulties.

In 1994, Robert had left the civil service and with a few business partners had bought a rundown hotel in the Welsh seaside resort of Barry. They refurbished it and reopened it as a nightclub, the Power Station. It was a successful business, which attracted a good weekend clubbing crowd from Cardiff.

In 1997, the nightclub was sold, and Robert reinvested his profits into a small 22-bedroom hotel, the Pembroke House Hotel in Haverfordwest the county town of Pembrokeshire, Wales. Business wise it was a disastrous decision and became, for Robert, a financial millstone. Robert tried to sell the hotel on a couple of occasions, but each time it failed to make its reserve price of £150,000.

A fire in the kitchens in January of 1999 closed the hotel down for good. There ensued a dispute with the insurance company, who ultimately refused to pay out. However, to friends and neighbours, Robert appeared as a successful businessman: his home was worth a lot of money and the teenagers' bedrooms were filled with all the latest gadgets.

Meanwhile, Robert's wife, Catherine, sister of the former Welsh rugby star Terry Holmes, was attending Cardiff University as a mature student studying for a degree in philosophy and sociology. She was also the secretary of the local parent-teacher association at St. Richard Gwyn Catholic School, which Sian and Luke attended. Catherine also regularly attended St. Helen's Catholic Church as well as Salsa classes with her best friend Debbie Zeraschi. Debbie, who lived close by, had children of similar ages to Robert's and Catherine's, and the families were close.

At the time of the appalling tragedy, **6ft tall** James, the eldest son, had just completed his sixth-form at St. David's Catholic College in Cardiff. It turned out later that he had passed enough A-levels to study law at Bristol University. While he was awaiting his results, he and some schoolmates had formed a band. Sian was awaiting her GCSEs results and was due to start at six form college the following September.

The youngest son, Luke, who was also **6ft tall**, was an avid snooker player and a Manchester United football supporter. Bethan, the youngest daughter, was autistic and attended a special-needs school in Barry. Her favourite activity was taking the family boxer dog, Brandy, walking around the neighbourhood.

Shortly before the massacre, Catherine had graduated at Cardiff University, and Robert had told a friend that "his wife's graduation as a mature student was one of the proudest days of his life."

Catherine surrounded by her proud husband and children at her graduation.

On the evening of July 19, Robert drove

Catherine and her best friend Debbie into Cardiff for a graduation party and later on in the evening picked them up at Barry train station. Catherine and Debbie met or spoke every day. On July 11, the two women attended a salsa class together. When they returned home at around 11:00 p.m., Debbie dropped Catherine off outside her £250,000 house and Catherine, as she climbed out of the car, said to Debbie,

"Bye, see you tomorrow."

It was the last time Debbie saw her friend alive.

The following day around noon, Debbie received a text message from Catherine calling off their arrangement to go to a parent-teacher meeting early that evening. She said it was because her mother was ill and would talk later. Debbie called Catherine but received no reply.

Normally, the Mochrie family home in Rutland Close was a hive of activity with teenagers coming and going. In the days following the text message to Debbie, it was as silent as a grave. It seemed to have been abandoned. Debbie phoned the house several times and sent text messages as well as knocking on the door. She was becoming more and more anxious as to where the family that she loved were.

By Sunday, July 23, Debbie, by now exceedingly worried, visited the house with a friend. When she saw Robert's car in the garage, her anxiety heightened as Robert never put it in the garage. She then began to notice a bad smell and flies. Looking in the downstairs windows of the house, although deserted, it looked as normal. With the help of her friend, Debbie got a ladder and climbed to the upstairs window of Luke's room. Peering in the window, she saw a shape lying motionless in bed. She immediately called the police.

When the police arrived at 8:30 p.m., it was dark. They forced their way into the house through the kitchen door. Everything downstairs seemed normal for a family home, with the clutter of teenage trainers in the hallway and James's guitar propped up against the sitting-room wall. The only thing out of place was a bucket and mop left in the kitchen and the dreadful smell pervading the house.

As the police ascended the stairs to the upstairs rooms, they found on the landing space a male adult hanging by his neck from rope suspended from the attic space above. Upon looking into one of the bedrooms, the police saw, protruding from under a duvet on a bed, a discolored arm.

The police left the house and sealed it as a crime scene and called in the murder squad and forensics.

The murder detectives and forensics found Catherine, dressed in her night clothes, in the marital bed bludgeoned to death. All of the children were found in their separate bedrooms in a similar state: bludgeoned to death, while lying on their stomachs, with their arms by their sides. The children's faces had all been turned to face the wall. There were no indications that any of the victims had put up a struggle. Spattered blood stained the walls, headboards, floors, and furniture of each bedroom. All of the bodies were in an advanced state of decomposition. They had been dead for around 10 days in the heat of July. Furthermore, the duvets, according to the forensic scientist, appeared to have been placed over each body after they had been killed. Detectives concluded that Robert, a seemingly loving husband and devoted father, had wielded eighteen blows to wipe out his family before killing himself.

It was now their job to try to determine why. To the police, it appeared to have been a pre-planned, methodical, and controlled act.

During the inquest into the deaths, the court heard that after Robert had bludgeoned his family to death, he left a note for the milkman stating: "No milk until Friday." He then took a mop and bucket from the kitchen up to his daughter Sian's room and cleaned up some blood that had sprayed on the wall behind her bed before covering her with a duvet cover. He then visited his other children's and wife's rooms and similarly tucked them up with duvets. At 5:30a.m., he phoned the school bus driver and left a message informing her that his youngest daughter, Bethan, 10, would be absent from school for the rest of the week.

At midday, he sent a text message from his wife's mobile/cell phone to Debbie, her best friend, cancelling their arrangement for that evening to attend a parent-teachers' association meeting. He then let the family boxer dog, Brandy, loose and put the cat out.

At some point after that, he swallowed a mixture of slug pellets, paracetamol, and weed killer. He then climbed up into the attic, placed a plastic bag over his head, took a rope, and made and placed a noose around his neck before jumping down into the landing below to his death.

The detectives had discovered during the course of their enquiries that Robert was facing bankruptcy. He had just £138 left in his business account and just £600 in his personal accounts. He was two months in arrears with his mortgage and behind with electricity and other household bills. At the time of his death, he owed a total of £200,000. It was not known if

Catherine was aware of their financial situation or not.

It also emerged during the inquest that Catherine had had a brief affair, which had ended five months before her murder. The affair had been with the hotel manager, David Osborne, of her husband's hotel. There was no evidence to suggest that Robert was aware of the affair.

At the time of her murder, Catherine had struck up a new relationship with Paul Wyatt, a man she had met in a pub. Again, there was no evidence presented that Robert knew of the friendship.

At the time of his wife's affairs, Robert, according to a prostitute, Charmaine Jacobs, visited her regularly twice a week for two years for masturbation. She said that Robert had told her that he and his wife no longer had sexual relations.

Deborah Zeraschi, Catherine's best friend, told the court that Robert was a "good friend, a good man, a loving husband and father." There was "never any physical violence" in the family and "Rob was one of the least aggressive people I have ever known."

Dr. Lawrence Addicott, the Cardiff and Vale coroner, recorded a verdict that Robert Mochrie unlawfully killed his family at their home in Barry, near Cardiff, and a verdict of suicide on Robert Mochrie.

FRANK FAIRLESS

In 2000, a self-employed builder Frank Fairless, 36, whose wife Claire had left him six months previously, suffocated his two sons, Christopher, 9 and Oliver, 6 and then hanged himself in his garage.

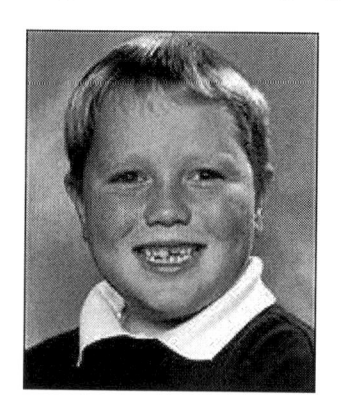

FRANK FAIRLESS

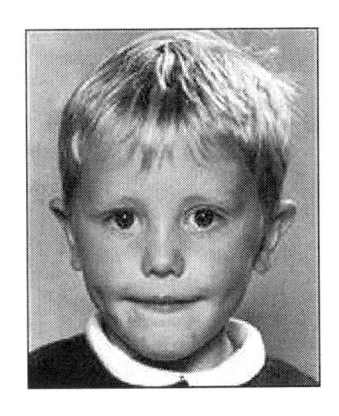

Christopher and Oliver

The boys' mother alerted the police when Frank had failed to return the boys at the agreed time on a Sunday evening.

The boys' bodies were discovered in their separate bedrooms lying in their beds at Olverchris Cottage, the family's former home, in the village of Scotter, Lincolnshire. It was their first overnight stay with their father since access had been agreed in the divorce courts.

KARL BLUESTONE

On Tuesday August 28, 2001, a police officer, Karl Bluestone, 36, murdered his pregnant wife, Jill Bluestone, 31, and their two young sons, Henry, 3, and Chandler, just 18-months-old, in Gravesend, Kent before hanging himself.

At around 10:00 p.m. on the evening of August 28, 2001, Ernest Lane heard a frantic knocking on his door. Leaving his sitting room, he went to investigate. Through the glass door, he saw his next-door neighbor's little girl, Jessica Bluestone, 6, dressed in her pajamas, and looking terrified. He hurriedly opened the door to her.

She said to him,

"My daddy is hitting my mommy. Please call the

police. Daddy banged my head on the wooden floor. I cannot get mommy out of my mind. She had blood coming out of her neck. I don't want daddy to kill mommy."

Ernest hurriedly telephoned the police.

The police quickly arrived on the scene and while a policewoman went to talk to Ernest Lane and Jessica, others went next door to the Bluestone's adjoining semi-detached three-bedroom house in Marling Way, Gravesend. In the driveway, the family's Mitsubishi Shogun was parked. The first officers to arrive at the family home at about 10:30 p.m. found Jill Bluestone's body on the kitchen floor. She had 13 hammer wounds to her head and a neck injury caused by the claw end of a hammer. Lying beside her was a blood-covered hammer.

At the foot of the stairs, Henry, the couple's three-year-old son, lay dead in his pajamas in a pool of blood. He had 10 hammer wounds to his head. Injuries to his hands indicated to police that he had desperately tried to protect himself.

Upstairs, the police found 18-month-old Chandler in his crib alive but with severe head injuries. He had endured six blows to his forehead. He was rushed to the hospital but died later that night at Darent Valley hospital in Dartford. The Bluestone's eldest child, Jack, 7, was discovered on the bottom bunk in his bedroom. He was lying in the fetal position, severely injured, but alive. He survived.

In the garage at the back of the house, Karl Bluestone, 36, was found hanging from a rope. On his arms, there were several marks, which the police believed were caused by his wife putting up a desperate fight for her life.

Karl Bluestone was born in 1965 to two Labour Councillors in Gravesend Kent. He joined the Kent Police Force in 1987. To his colleagues in the force he was a "fun-loving professional," who loved his children.

KARL BLUESTONE

Karl Bluestone

To his wife, Jill, he was a controlling abusive husband who had affairs with other women.

During the course of their stormy marriage, he had kicked Jill in the stomach whilst she was pregnant, threatened her with a meat cleaver, and on another occasion had smashed the back window of her Mercedes.

In June of 1999, Karl was arrested over a violent argument with his wife. During the row, Jessica, then five, was accidentally injured by a vase that Karl had hurled at Jill before he throttled his wife until she lost consciousness.

He was not charged after the incident as Jill refused to press charges.

During the month of August of 2001, Karl became increasingly irate and started to record Jill's telephone calls as he had become convinced that Jill, who worked for Basildon District Council as a senior manager, was having an affair with a work colleague.

Unable to take the jealousy and abuse any longer Jill told her husband on August 25th that she wanted to leave the marriage and take the children with her.

Jill told a friend that she felt increasingly fearful for her life; that Karl had said to her when she talked about ending the marriage,

"There is no divorce – the only way out is death."

On the day that Karl murdered his wife and two youngest children and the attempted murder of his eldest two children, he had joined work colleagues from the Windmill Street Police Station in Gravesend for an after-work drink before returning to the family home. Here, he settled in front of the television to watch one of his favorite programs, the police drama *The Bill*.

After the program finished, he began a blazing row with his wife, which culminated in the appalling tragedy.

The Inquest

In November of 2001, an inquest was held into the murders in Gravesend County Court, in front of Coroner Roger Hatch. The coroner, after hearing all the evidence, said in his summing up that Karl Bluestone had realized his marriage was over and said,

"Whilst it cannot explain the tragedy, it perhaps gives an insight into Karl Bluestone's mind on August 28th."

He recorded verdicts of the unlawful killing for Jill Bluestone, 31, Henry, 3, and Chandler, 1, with head injuries being the cause of death. He recorded a verdict of suicide for Karl Bluestone, 36.

Bluestone children

The two surviving children, Jessica and Jack, were taken in by relatives. How they can ever come to terms with the nightmare of that night is hard to imagine.

STEVEN WILSON

Denise Williams was born in 1976 into a dysfunctional family in Birmingham, the most populous UK city outside the British capital of London, England. When she was 16, she met 18-stone (252 pounds) former soldier, Steven Wilson, age 35, a widower whose first wife had died from cancer shortly before they met. He was now a single father of a son, Konrad and a daughter, Stacey. Steven had impressed the vulnerable young Denise by boasting of his time in the SAS, the English elite special armed forces. Shortly after meeting him, she became pregnant, and they married a week before her 17th birthday in 1993. She moved into his home in Linden Avenue, Great Barr, Birmingham.

On October 26th, 1993, Denise gave birth to their son Bret. Ten months later, she gave birth to another son, Brad Lee. Denise's dream was to create a happy, loving, secure family unit that she herself had never had but had desperately yearned for.

Within a short amount of time, Denise realized her husband was a heavy drinker and a violent bully. As the marriage progressed, the violence became worse. She found her husband to be a Jekyll and Hyde type character. When he wasn't drinking too much, there were good times, nice holidays, and family outings. However, the good times were short lived. The only real thing that Denise derived pleasure from was her adored sons, Brett and Bradley. On a number of occasions when badly beaten, she would flee the house to a hostel for battered women with her small sons dressed in their pajamas and clutching their teddy bears. However, her husband always found them. He would be sitting outside the hostel in his car waiting for them and after apologies and persuasion or threats from

Steve, they would all return home.

On a couple of occasions, she was hospitalized by his beatings: once when he broke her nose with a head-butt and, on another occasion, he had flung pool balls with such force at her knee caps that she was barely able to walk. On each occasion, she returned home because of her sons. She also returned because of Steve's threats that if she ever left him, he had good SAS friends who would track her down and that he would always find her and deal with her accordingly. Not knowing any better, she believed him. In fact, the truth was he had served just 138 days in the regular Army when he was 19 before being discharged in 1977 after fighting with other recruits.

As the boys became older, they, too, were subjected to abuse from their father. He would make them stand with their arms stretched out, holding heavy telephone directories. If their arms drooped, he'd force them back up again and again until they were reduced to tears from the pain. He would also make them lie down on the floor and raise their legs a few inches off of the floor until they were in pain. He would say that is what it was like in the SAS.

During the course of their marriage, Steven never worked but lived off the British Social Security System, which meant money was always tight. Because of the financial situation, he forced his wife, through violence and psychological bullying, into prostitution, a job she detested.

Steven, in a garden shed in the back garden, built a makeshift brothel decorated with a boar's head and crossed guns to apparently conjure up images of a log cabin in the Wild West. He filmed her having sex with one of her clients with which he further threatened her. All of her earnings were kept by him.

One night in February of 2002, after being subjected to another violent beating by her husband, Denise fled the house in the middle of the night as Steven lay in a drunken stupor on the floor of her son's bedroom. She was taken in by a friend whose address Steven didn't know. Denise left Bret and Brad behind.

It was a hasty decision she would live to regret for the rest of her life.

However, this time she was determined to leave for good and seek professional help and advice to reclaim her boys, as they were seeing too much violence and she had to get herself and them out before it was too late.

Four days after moving out, and after continual calls from Steven to her cell phone and desperately missing her sons, she agreed to meet Steven and the boys on February 6th in a McDonald's restaurant in West Bromwich, Birmingham. Denise took a tram to McDonald's where Steven and her sons were waiting for her in the parking lot. She later recalled that the boys were overjoyed and relieved to see her. She found Steven to be irritable with the boys and oddly behaved with a dead look in his eyes. They, however, managed to have a peaceful meal with their sons.

After the meal Steven said he would like to talk. They walked back to the car and settled the boys in the back seat. Standing outside of the car, Denise summoned up the courage to tell Steven she was not returning to him ever again, that things had gone too far, and it had to stop. She told him that the boys could stay with him while she sorted out new accommodations for them.

He pleaded with her to return home and if she didn't he threatened her that he would kill the kids. She stayed resolute in her resolve, not taking his threat seriously. Steven Wilson then turned murderously violent. He pulled his wife towards him and began punching her really hard in the side of her head, causing the rings on his fingers to slice into her skin. Her horrified sons looked on. He left her laying in a bloody mess sprawled on the floor of the parking lot before jumping into his four wheel-drive Daihatsu. As he screeched off in the car, Steven, with his sons in the back seat, attempted to run over his wife.

Denise, battered, bloodied, bruised, and shaken managed to get the tram back to her friend's apartment, knowing that she urgently needed to get Brett and

Bradley away from their abusive father.

As she walked into her friend's apartment, her cell phone rang. It was Steven. His message was short.

"I've just killed the kids, and I'm going to kill myself."

He then hung up the phone. Denise, panic struck, rushed out to the street and ran to the nearest police station, thinking as she ran, *'there's no way he'd do that.'* She would not allow herself to believe it.

Entering the police station, still in a bloody and disheveled state, she called out to the policeman on duty,

"My husband has phoned to say he's killed our children!"

The police immediately took her seriously for they, too, had just received a similar call from Steven, but he would not disclose where he was. Denise was led to a waiting room while the police began a search. She still kept telling herself that he would not seriously have killed the boys. As she sat in the waiting room, she could hear a search helicopter and people racing around. Denise was sure they'd find the boys and bring them to her.

After Steven had driven off from the McDonald's parking lot, he drove to Handsworth Golf Club. Although situated only a few miles from Birmingham City Centre, the golf course had tree-lined fairways and gently undulating greens. Here, Steven parked his car behind some outbuildings in an area that was dark, lonely, isolated, and secluded.

Grabbing a craft knife and a screwdriver from the glove compartment, and still seething with fury, Steven climbed into the back seat of the car beside his sons. He raised the knife and slashed seven-year-old Bradley's throat with such force that his knife broke; he then stabbed him with the screwdriver puncturing the carotid arteries, so he was dead within minutes.

Eight-year-old Brett watched on in horror as his young brother was being murdered. He vomited. Steven then turned his attention to Brett, who in all likelihood attempted to defend himself against his father, who beat him across the face, neck, and arms before stabbing him in the throat four times with the same screwdriver he had used to kill Brad.

Steven then phoned Denise and in a 12-second phone call told her what he had done. He then made three 999 (911) calls telling the operators he had 'killed the kids' and he was ' going to kill himself.'

In one phone call to the emergency phone operators, he said that his wife was a prostitute and if the police looked above his bed, they would find a video of his wife working as a prostitute. In all of the calls, he refused to disclose his location.

He also telephoned his eldest son Konrad and confessed the murders to him. He then stabbed himself in the chest with the screwdriver but suffered only superficial wounds.

At 2201 GMT, on the night of February 6th of 2002, the police helicopter spotted 44-year-old Steven Wilson's Daihatsu vehicle. His slumped body was found resting over his dead sons.

***

A police officer went into the waiting room where Denise had been anxiously waiting for well over two-hours and somberly told her,

"Denise, we've found the boys."

She was overjoyed and asked how long it would be until they arrived at the station. He told her they wouldn't be coming to the station as Steven had killed them. She slapped the police officer and then collapsed into unconsciousness.

When she regained consciousness, a doctor asked if there was anything he could give her and she replied, "A lethal injection."

Following an autopsy, the two boys' bodies were taken to a chapel of rest where every day before their funeral Denise sat with them from 9a.m. to 5p.m. She showered Brett's and Bradley's bodies and dressed them before their funeral. She considered suicide constantly. The fear they must have felt before their deaths haunted her. They were the reasons she had put up with the years of horrific abuse from her husband. Without them, she felt her life was over and that her heart had been ripped out.

In her nightmares, she would see the look of terror that must have been on their faces when Steven killed them. In the following weeks, Denise's mental state plunged into a deep black hole where she drank a 75 liter bottle of whisky a day. She felt totally lost and suicidal.

At the funeral, where she was supported by her police liaison officer, an old family friend, Kevin Griffiths, told her that if she wanted to talk, to give him a call.

Denise, in desperation, phoned Kevin one day. He became her lifeline and the relationship very quickly became one of more than friends. They became lovers, and she became pregnant with a son: Owen.

***

THE TRIAL

Four months after Owen's birth, in March of 2003, Steven Wilson's trial was held at Birmingham Crown Court. Despite his having confessed to his wife and the emergency phone operators, Steven Wilson entered a plea of not guilty to all charges.

During the 13-day trial, Steven Wilson, giving evidence from the witness box, claimed that his wife Denise had set Albanian gangsters on to him as payback for an alleged theft of cash and cocaine from a brothel that his wife managed. He cried and clung to a large crucifix hanging around his neck as he vividly described how the Albanians had butchered Brad and Brett in front of him, even imitating the accent of one of the supposed gang members.

Denise, then age 26, had reverted to her maiden name of Williams. She told the court about her devastation at losing her sons and revealed her horrific life of torment with her bullying and sadistic husband.

Stacey Banner, Steven Wilson's daughter by his

first wife, testified that she had left home in January of 2001 because of her father's abusive behavior, which included "mind games" and "weekly" violence meted out to anyone who angered him. She also said that her father controlled the household by fear and would frequently slap Brad and Brett.

The prosecutor, David Crigman QC, told the court,

"He must have been seething that he could no longer control his wife and didn't even know where she was living."

David Crigman continued,

"His venom against Denise was such that he was determined to teach her a lesson she would never forget. He took the ultimate revenge by killing their children."

The jury took just 50 minutes to reach unanimous guilty verdicts on both charges of murder and a further charge of assaulting Denise Williams on the same night in February of 2002.

The judge gave him two life sentences for his "dreadful and wicked" crime with a concurrent 12-month sentence for attacking his wife.

Steven Wilson

Following the court case, Steven Wilson's estranged parents said,

"We are disgusted, appalled, and ashamed of Steven committing this cowardly attack against two small boys, but we are not surprised. He is an evil, lying, controlling, manipulative, and devious bully who is also power and money-mad."

His daughter, Stacey Banner, told journalists

that he should never be allowed to walk the streets again.

On March 30th, six days into his sentence, Steven Wilson was found hanged by his shoelaces in his cell at Blakenhurst prison in Redditch, Worcestershire.

His daughter-in-law was reported to have said,

"At least now there is no way he can ever hurt again the people he has caused so much pain to over the years, and I am delighted that he is no longer able to intimidate, manipulate, or bully anyone. It is the best thing that could have happened. The rest of his family can at last sleep easy."

A former neighbor of his said,

"I have known him since 1966, since he was a little boy. He was a horrible kid. My kids were always petrified of going out when he was around. He was just a nasty evil man. I am so glad we have seen the last of him."

Denise Williams and Kevin Griffiths married in 2005. Her police liaison officer gave her away. In 2006, they had a daughter Katie and four years later in 2010 they had another daughter, Grace. They live with their three children in a terraced house in Birmingham. She says her sons Brad and Brett are with her all the time in her head and in her heart.

She still has bad days when she goes into the bedroom and lies down and cries. She says,

"I can't stop the flashbacks and the nightmares, but I cope. I deal with it. I appreciate every moment with Kevin and our children and treasure every memory of Brett and Bradley."

KEITH YOUNG

Keith Young, 38, a farm labourer from Winsford, Cheshire killed his four sons Joshua, seven, Thomas, six, Callum, five, and Daniel, three, in March of 2003 before killing himself. Keith and the boy's mother, Samantha Tolley, had endured a long and stormy relationship. Despite being assaulted several times by her husband, once sustaining a broken wrist, and stays in women's shelters, Samantha kept returning to her husband, who she had married in June of 2001 for the sake of the children. Towards the end of 2002, she left him for good and moved with the boys from

Winsford to nearby Weaverham.

Despite leaving Keith, she allowed him almost unrestricted access to the children. She thought he was a good father, just not a good husband, and it never occurred to her that he would harm the boys in any way.

Despite his freedom of access to the boys, he became increasingly depressed over the breakdown of the marriage. He told friends and relatives that he felt like gassing himself and the boys. No one took him seriously, as he was regarded as a happy-go-lucky man who doted on his sons.

On Wednesday March 27, the boys were spending the night with Keith at his house in Winsford. Earlier that day or the previous day Keith had learned that Samantha, his estranged wife, was pregnant by another man. Later that evening after the boys had gone to bed, he went and woke them and ushered them all into the back seat of his Mitsubishi Shogun - still dressed in their pajamas. In the front passenger seat, he had placed a petrol fuelled lawn mower.

He then drove them all to Horseshoe Pass, a beautiful lookout spot near Llangollen, North Wales. From here, at around 12.30 a.m., he telephoned his estranged wife and told her he was about to kill the boys and himself with fumes from his garden lawnmower. She asked him where he was, but he refused to say before hanging up.

Terrified and totally frantic, she called the police and her brother. The police began desperately to attempt to trace the location from which the call was made. Shortly afterwards, Keith called her again and said he had started the lawnmower and added,

"I hope you're happy - I hope you have a grudge against that baby for the rest of your life."

Keith then asked her,

"Can you hear the mower?"

She replied, "Yes."

Then he asked, "Can you hear your children?"

In the background, she could hear the children crying and coughing.

Samantha again answered "Yes" before the call was abruptly ended.

Keith telephoned again at about 1:15a.m., by which time her brother Steven and a police officer were with Samantha. She again begged him to tell her where he was. In desperation, she told him she would have an abortion and try to make their relationship work again. Keith replied,

"It's too late. Dan's dead."

In the background, she could hear her eldest son asking for her. She heard Keith telling him,

"Say goodbye to your mom and tell her you love her."

Joshua came on the line and obediently said goodbye to her and told her he loved her. She pleaded with Joshua to say where they were. He replied,

"It's too dark - it's smoky."

Keith then took the phone back from Joshua, and Samantha begged him to stop the madness. Keith replied,

"It's one down. I've got to go through with it. I've gone too far. I'll go to jail. I've got to do it."

Keith then informed her that another of her sons had died, followed shortly afterwards by a third. He then told her he was feeling tired, his nose had started bleeding, and he was suffering from pins and needles.

"Isn't it funny - getting a nosebleed before you die," he said to Samantha.

Samantha then heard Keith breathing heavily for a while, followed by total and complete silence. She remained on the line for about twenty minutes, crying, and occasionally shouting hoping to get some sort of reaction from her sons or estranged husband.

When she heard the police arriving at her husband's vehicle at about 2:00 a.m., she passed the phone over to the police officer.

Later that night, the distraught mother, Samantha Tolley, identified the bodies of her four dead sons.

INQUEST

In September of 2003, an inquest was held into the deaths in Wrexham, North Wales in front of coroner John Hughes. A pathologist told the court that Keith Young and his four young sons had all died from carbon monoxide poisoning. The pathologist said in his opinion the boys would not have suffered, as they would have become drowsy and fallen asleep.

Thomas, Callum, Daniel and Joshua,

Samantha Tolley, giving evidence, had to again endure the horrific events of the tragic night in March of 2003.

In his summing up, the coroner, John Hughes, said he believed Keith Young's actions were triggered by Samantha, his wife, becoming pregnant. Following the events of that night, Samantha Tolley lost her baby.

The coroner returned verdicts of unlawful killing on the four boys and one of suicide on their father. He said it was one of the most harrowing cases he had ever dealt with.

Following the inquest, Samantha's Tolley's lawyer, Sarah Lapsley, said her client would never get over the tragedy. She said,

"While the boys' suffering has ended, their mother's torment continues on a daily basis and will do so for the rest of her life."

JAYA PRAKASH CHITI

On a cold winter morning on February 1, 2004, at around 4:00 a.m., a motorist saw a Toyota Corolla parked with its hazard lights flashing on the westbound carriageway of the Orwell Bridge just south of Ipswich in Suffolk, England.

The Orwell Bridge and the Clifton Suspension Bridge in Bristol have the unenviable title of Britain's favorite suicide spots. The motorist, feeling concerned, telephoned the police. Within a short time, police officers arrived at the scene. One officer, on opening the driver's door, noticed what he believed to be blood on the steering wheel, the driver's seat, and the gear shift of the car.

Another officer, looking over the side of the

bridge, noticed what looked like a body lying on a concrete block at the base of the bridge. The officers called for other emergency services and more police officers to join them.

Orwell Suspension Bridge

At the foot of the bridge, the body of Jaya Prakash Chiti, 41, was found and close by partially in the freezing water the coastguards found the body of his two-year-old son Pranau.

The police identified the car as belonging to a doctor and registered at an address in a village just three

DEADLY DADS OF THE UK

miles north-east of the center of Ipswich.

Detectives made their way to the address that was situated in Seckford Close, Rushmere St Andrew, which was two miles from the Orwell Bridge. It was a large, four-bedroom, detached modern house in a quiet cul-de-sac with a Toyota Yaris hatchback parked in the drive. The house was in darkness. Receiving no reply to their knocks on the door, the police entered the $402,000 home.

Upstairs in the main bedroom, they discovered the dead body of Jaya Chiti's wife, Dr. Anupama Damera, 36. She had been stabbed and slashed multiple times by two separate kitchen knives. Detectives, upon examination of the room, believe that Dr. Chiti had threatened and taunted his wife, slashing her body multiple times before killing her with two fatal stab wounds to the chest.

Two blood-stained kitchen knives and copies of email correspondence between Anupama and a former colleague of hers, Dr. Dunn, a radiologist at the

Queen's Medical Centre in Nottingham, were found nearby.

In a separate bedroom in the house, the police discovered the couple's eldest son, 11-year-old Ani, asleep in his bed unharmed and unaware of the horror that had taken place whilst he slept.

The Chitis were originally from India where they had both qualified as doctors. They had married on December 30, 1988. It was an arranged marriage. In 1992, they had their first son, Ani.

In 1996, Anupama moved to Nottingham in England to train in radiology at the Queen's Medical Centre and become a breast cancer specialist. Dr. Chiti and Ani soon joined her. In February of 2001, the couple had their second son, Pranau.

In 2003, Anupama was offered an $80,000 -a-year job as a consultant radiologist at Ipswich Hospital, Suffolk. The family moved to their house in Rushmere St. Andrew in August of 2003. Dr. Chiti took a temporary job in the accident and emergency department at the Hospital. He was due to start a new job as a senior houseman a few days after his death.

In January of 2004, Dr. Chiti returned to Nizamabad, India to visit his family. He returned to the United Kingdom late in January. Detectives investigating the deaths discovered that at the end of January, Dr. Chiti had emptied all of the money out of a number of bank accounts and stored the balance in one joint account. He also collected together various pieces of jewellery and gold which he posted to a family friend asking for it to be distributed among his sister's and brother's children. The package arrived at the friend's house the day following his death.

An inquest into the deaths was held in July of 2004 at the Ipswich Crown Court in front of Peter Dean, a Suffolk coroner.

Detective Superintendent Lambert, who led the investigations into the deaths, was the first to give evidence. He told the court about the money transfers and parcel. He also told the court about what he believed was the significance of the printed out emails found along with Anupama's body.

He said they had Dr. Chiti's fingerprints on them. The emails were between Anupama and Dr. William Dunn, a married man with a thirteen year old daughter, who was a former colleague of hers at the Queen's Medical Centre in Nottingham. Detective Supt Lambert said it would be fair for anyone reading them to assume that there relationship was "more than professional." The detective believed that Dr. Chiti, after reading the emails, was convinced that his wife and Dr. Dunn were having an affair and was consumed by jealousy. Detective Superintendent Lambert said that,

"Anupama often confided to her colleagues about her sadness at being within an arranged marriage and her desire to leave this relationship."

Dr. Dunn was called to the inquest to give evidence. He told the jury that Anupama had confided she was unhappy about her arranged marriage. He said:

"I knew her for a long time, and she told me a lot of things over the years. We had a lot of conversations on the phone and through email. She confided in me a lot of details about her marriage and how she felt about it."

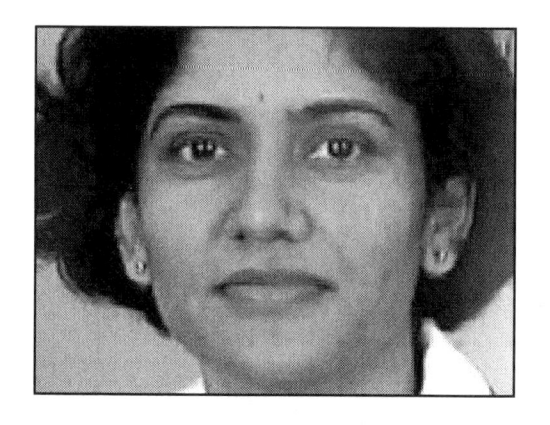

Anupama Damera

Dr. Dunn was not asked directly if he had had an affair with Anupama and after giving evidence he left through a side door without commenting to reporters, and the emails were never read out loud in court.

JAYA PRAKASH CHITI

In his summing up, the Suffolk Coroner said the emptying of the bank accounts and the posting of the package,

"Would seem to suggest the possibility of Dr. Chiti's actions being premeditated."

He also said that,

"If Jaya Chiti had read those [e-mails], he may have developed the perception that there may have been more than a friendship going on."

He recorded verdicts of unlawful killing on the deaths of Anupama and Pranau and a verdict of suicide on Jaya Chiti.

At the end of the hearing, Ashok Damera, Anupama's brother, in a statement read to the court said,

"We all have problems, and we need to work them out. Killing your spouse or innocent children is not an option. For heaven's sake talk to someone, get a divorce, or share child custody. Do not ever resort to this horrific act of taking the life of your own family, your own flesh and blood."

RICHARD HICKS

As two teenage twin sisters walked home on a dark chilly evening at around 6:40 p.m. on February 3rd, 2004, they heard the sound of a child crying from what appeared to be an abandoned blue Nissan Micra car parked close to the Humber Suspension Bridge in Barton, North Lincolnshire.

Looking into the back of the car, they saw a distressed baby girl of about thirteen months old strapped into a child seat. One of the twins phoned her mother, while the other attempted to soothe the child. The twin's mother called the police who rapidly appeared on the scene.

Social Services took the baby into care while police officers traced the owner of the vehicle to 33-year-old Joanne Catley who resided at Webster Mews in

Healing, Lincolnshire.

The police traveled to the address 20 miles away and upon not receiving any answer to their knocks on the door, entered the unlocked end-of-terrace house. What greeted them in the kitchen was what Detective Chief Inspector Phil Spicksley later described as a "horrific crime scene." Police found Joanne Catley and her two young daughters Phoebe, four, and Emma, two, stabbed violently and viciously to death from multiple stab wounds in the kitchen. Joanne, Phoebe, and Emma also had injuries to their hands believed to be caused by attempting to defend themselves.

A search warrant was immediately put out for Joanne's ex-partner and father of the girls, 37-year-old Richard Hicks.

Later that night, river police found Richard Hicks's body partially submerged in the Humber River on a concrete platform 60ft below the Humber suspension bridge. Post mortem tests on his body showed he had died from multiple injuries, which were consistent with a fall, and that he had almost three times the legal limit of alcohol for driving in his body. The Humberside police said they were treating the case as a triple murder and suicide.

Baby Lily was released from Social Services and placed in the care of her maternal grandparents, Aldrene and John, who were in deep shock at the death of their daughter and grandchildren and who were being comforted by their son David and other family members at their home in Grimsby.

Phoebe, Emma and Baby Lily

Joanne Catley had been brought up in the seaport of Grimsby on the Humber Estuary in

Lincolnshire, north-east England. In the mid-90s, she moved south to London where she managed a pub. It was here that she met and fell in love with Richard Hicks, who also worked in the pub.

Richard Hicks at a party.

In 1999, after their first child Phoebe was born, the couple moved to north-east England to be near her parents and brother in Grimsby. Joanne became the manager of the Green Man Pub in the small village of Stallingborough. They lived over the bar in a staff apartment. Stallingborough, despite its closeness to major industries and the populous seaport of Grimsby, was a small community in a rural setting.

Joanne was popular in the community and was described by friends as "popular and happy-go-lucky" and who doted on her children.

In 2003, the couple's relationship began to deteriorate. In August, Richard was arrested for fighting in a public place at London Euston railway station. He admitted to disturbing the peace and was sentenced to a 12-month rehabilitation order.

Richard became more and more aggressive towards Joanne, which culminated on the night of November 22nd, 2003 when Richard allegedly grabbed Joanne's face and bit her nose, drawing blood. Joanne called the police, who charged him with common assault. It was the second time in less than a month that Joanne had had to call the police on him. This time, she applied for and was granted a restraining order against him. On November 25, 2003, he pleaded not guilty to the offence, and Grimsby magistrates granted him bail on condition that he did not communicate or interfere with Joanne. The pre-trial hearing was scheduled for February 19th, 2004 at Grimsby Magistrates' Court.

Upon release, Richard rented an apartment in Grimsby and got work as the kitchen restaurant manager in the Haven pub. Friends later said he had been totally devastated by the family break-up as Joanne was his one true love. Another friend said that Richard was a devoted father whose eyes lit up when he talked about his daughters, who were his princesses. A regular client at The Haven was later to tell a reporter that,

"He lived for his kids and talked about them non-stop."

Despite the impending court case, Joanne dropped the restraining order preventing Richard from access to their daughters and would take the girls into the pub where he worked so that they could see their father. No doubt, Joanne felt safer in an environment where there were other people.

In January of 2004, Joanne resigned her position at The Green Man so she could spend more time with her children and moved to the nearby small village of Healing.

Word reached Richard in late January that Joanne had begun seeing someone else, Robert Park, age 52, a shipping worker who lived in Rugby, Warwickshire. Richard told friends that he would kill both of them if he discovered they had had sex.

On February 3, 2004, Richard, enraged by jealousy, made his way to Joanne's house in Healing. On the way, he stopped at a shop and bought a kitchen knife with an eight-inch blade for $37. When he arrived at the house, it was empty. Joanne had left home to pick four-year-old Phoebe up from the village school. He hid and waited. He did not have to wait long before Joanne arrived back home. As she helped Phoebe and lifted Emma out of the car, he made his appearance and forced them into the house and into the kitchen, leaving baby Lily still strapped into her car seat.

Once he had them in the kitchen, his anger took over. He stabbed Joanne seventy times in front of their two terrified daughters before turning on them. Two year old Emma was stabbed thirty-two times and four year old Phoebe suffered 26 bruises and stab wounds. One of the wounds which penetrated her heart was eight inches deep

Richard then left the blood soaked knife on the kitchen table, the tip of its blade bent by the force of the frenzied and ferocious attack. Before leaving the house, he took Joanne's phone from her bag.

Covered and dripping with blood, Richard left the house and drove Joanne's car with baby Lily still in the back twenty miles to the Humber Bridge where he parked. He then dialed Robert Park's number but got no answer. Abandoning the phone, he climbed out of the car and leapt to his death.

In July of 2004 an inquest was held into the deaths.

Coroner David Overton, after hearing all the evidence, told the hearing that Richard Hicks had apparently become jealous about Joanne Catley seeing someone else and that the attacks were clearly pre-planned. He said that Mr. Hicks was filled with feelings of "possessiveness, bitterness, and revenge" and that he was motivated by the determination that if he couldn't have his family, no one could.

Commenting on Phoebe and Emma witnessing their mother's death, he said,

"What went through their minds at this stage is unimaginable."

Coroner David Overton recorded that Joanne and her daughters were unlawfully killed and that Richard Hicks took his own life.

Aldrene Catley, Joanne's mother, following the inquest said,

"My daughter and grandchildren will be in my heart and mind for the rest of my life."

Detective Chief Inspector Sharon Fielding, who led the investigation into the killings, said,

"It is difficult to find the words to describe the

utter tragedy of those events."

GAVIN HALL

In October of 2005 when Gavin Hall, 33, a hospital radiographer, discovered his wife, Joanne, 31, was having an affair, he was filled with anguish.

Joanne had begun an affair with James Muir-Little, 45, a married father of two and part-time judge.

They had met on an Internet site for married people in September of 2005. They exchanged photographs of themselves naked and described in explicit detail fantasies of what they wanted to do with each other. In one email exchange, Joanne said she would be his "dirty little slut." The couple met twice for sex in hotels in Northampton, 11 miles south of the village of Irchester, where Joanne lived with Gavin and their two young daughters, Amelia - known as Millie, 3, and Lucy, 1, and their two cats.

When Gavin confronted his wife after discovering the emails, Joanne reassured him that it was just a fling, and it was over. Following the revelation of his wife's affair, Gavin became depressed and was prescribed anti-depressants.

Towards the end of November of 2005, Gavin discovered text messages between Joanne and James Muir-Little, who lived in Kent, and realized that, despite her reassurances to the contrary, the lovers were still in touch.

It was then that Gavin began to plot his deadly revenge on his wife. On the night of November 28, he killed the two family cats with chloroform and hid their bodies in a garden shed.

The following night in the early hours of November 29, when his wife was asleep in bed, Gavin went upstairs to his daughter's bedroom and woke Millie. He carried her downstairs to the living room. Here, the little girl sat on her Daddy's knee while he gave her one of his anti-depressant pills. When she began to get drowsy cuddled in his lap, Gavin took a Chloroform covered cloth and placed it over her mouth. Millie tried to push the cloth away that was burning the skin around her mouth and eyes but in vain as her father just pressed it onto her harder, his finger nails digging into her skin as she slowly died.

Amelia Hall

    He then began to prepare a scene of horror for his wife to find. He placed Millie's lifeless body on the living room floor. He then retrieved the dead cats from the shed and placed them next to her, along with her favorite teddy bear. He covered them all with a duvet.

Gavin then sent a text to his wife, who was still asleep with the baby Lucy upstairs, in which he explained he had taken Millie's life for revenge for her "deceit." He then sent his wife's lover a text to say that he also was to blame.

Gavin then set about trying to kill himself with the chloroform and slashed his wrists, neck, thighs, and arms.

The following morning as Joanne, a cardiac nurse, entered the living room with her baby Lucy in her arms, she found Gavin unconscious and bleeding heavily from cuts. It is hard to imagine what she felt or thought when she lifted the duvet on the floor.

She later described it as "a scene of pure horror."

Later, when Gavin had recovered in the hospital, he told police,

"I killed my angel, and I have not joined her."

He was arrested and charged with the murder of his three-year-old daughter.

The Trial

At Northampton Crown Court in 2006, Gavin Hall pleaded not guilty to murder but guilty to manslaughter due to an "abnormality of mind" after reading "sexually explicit" e-mails between his wife and James Muir-Little.

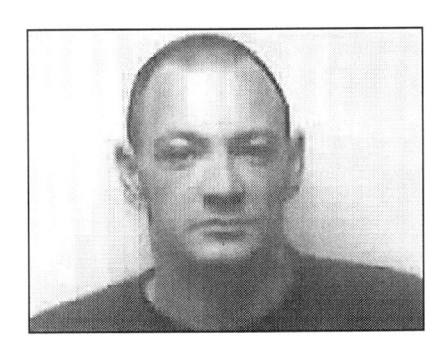

Gavin Hall

However, the jury, after a six-day trial, found him unanimously guilty of premeditated murder motivated by anger, bitterness, and revenge against his wife. As the jury read out their verdict, Gavin trembled and wept.

Before passing sentence, Judge Charles Wide

QC said to Gavin,

"It has been said, and it is true, that you will have to live for the rest of your life with what you did. Joanne will have to live for the rest of her life with what you did."

Gavin Hall was sentenced to life imprisonment with a minimum term of 15 years.

ROBERT THOMSON

Robert Thomson, 50, was a digger driver. He stabbed to death his Down Syndrome daughter Michelle, 25, and seven year old son Ryan in their bedrooms in the former family home in Muiredge Cottage, Buckhaven, Fife, Scotland, on May 3, 2008 before trying or pretending to attempt to kill himself.

His wife of 27 years, June, had left the marriage and former family home in March with their children Michelle and Ryan and was planning to start a new life in a new apartment in Markinch, a small town in Fife.

June had met Robert when she was 17. During the stormy marriage, she had attempted to leave her abusive and controlling husband on a number of occasions. She once ran away to Liverpool, but Robert hired a private detective who found her. Another time, after a night of abuse, she fled to a women's shelter where Robert tracked her down and brought her home. She finally decided to leave for good when he wanted to put Michelle into a home.

The day before the murders, there had been a preliminary divorce court hearing in which June was reportedly seeking an $80,000 divorce settlement and $400 weekly custody maintenance for the children.

On May 3, while she attended to various chores, June had left the two children in her estranged husband's care, their first official visitation with their father since the parents' separation. Robert and June, during their marriage, had four children between them. Their eldest son Shaun, 27, lived in Essex, England, and their son Ross, 20, still lived in the family home with his father.

After June had left the children in Robert's care and left the house, Robert gave his son Ross a shopping list of groceries he said he needed. At around 4:00 p.m., Ross departed the home on his errand. While Ross was out of the house, Robert Thomson, in separate bedrooms, stabbed his daughter Michelle 12 times and Ryan 14 times.

His son Ross returned from his shopping errand with his girlfriend, Kay Wallace. After putting the groceries away, they went to his bedroom upstairs to watch a DVD - unaware of the fate that had befallen his elder sister and younger brother.

June Thompson arrived back at the house at around seven in the evening. She made her way to Michelle's room where, to her horror, she saw her daughter's bloodied dead body. In total panic, she ran to Ryan's room and saw him lying in bed. She pulled back the bedclothes and saw blood on his stomach and stab wounds. June began screaming.

Her son Ross heard her screaming:

"He's killed them."

In the main bedroom, her husband was in bed pretending to be dead. A bloodied knife lay beside him. He had slashed both his wrists and stabbed himself in the stomach. On the bedside table was a suicide note which included a message to his wife,

"June - too much pain, lies, and hurt. Don't blame yourself. I will look after them. Just like your mother, move on alone. Love Rab XXX."

While the children's bodies were removed to the morgue, Robert Thompson was taken to Queen Margaret Hospital, Dunfermline. He was later charged with the murders of his two children.

At his subsequent trial, at the High Court in Edinburgh, he pleaded guilty and was sentenced to seventeen years in prison. He has never shown any remorse.

June Thompson, after the trial said,

"It wasn't long enough, 17 years. I think that is disgusting. For two beautiful children's lives, it's not long enough. He is an evil, sick, nasty, horrible man who is full of pure evil and badness. He has given me no answers why he did this. He stole their lives away from them."

ASHOK KALYANJEE

On the same day that Robert Thomson committed his heinous crimes, less than fifty miles away another father was committing a similar crime.

Indian born Ashok Kalyanjee and Giselle Ross (Scottish) married in 2001, and their first son Paul was born in November of 2001. Although they were married, they never lived together as Ashok preferred to live with his aging mother, Maya Devi, 70. They divorced three years later in 2004 because of Ashok's drinking and gambling problems. However, they still occasionally enjoyed close relations, and they had another son, Jay Ross, in January of 2006.

On May 3, 2008, Ashok, 41, telephoned his estranged wife Giselle and asked her if he could have their sons, Paul, 6, and Jay Ross, 2, for the afternoon to visit his mother and play football in the park. Giselle agreed.

On the way to Giselle's house in Royston, Glasgow, Ashok stopped and bought a large chef's knife and a can of petrol, which he placed in the trunk of his diesel Mercedes.

When he arrived at Giselle's house around midday, Paul was reluctant to go with his father, but Ashok gave him $16 to buy a Spiderman toy with. Ashok told his sons to bring their yellow football, as they were going to go to the park. As Ashok and the boys drove off Giselle waved them off, calling out,

"Bye babies."

Ashok did not take his sons to see their grandmother Maya nor did he take them to the park to play football. Instead, he took them to his ex-wife's favourite beauty spot from her childhood, Campsie Fells above Lennoxtown, tarnishing her favourite childhood memories forever.

At about 1:00 p.m. Ashok phoned Giselle and said to her,

"Your babies are fine. Your babies are fine."

Giselle thought his voice sounded "cold and strange."

Ashok then said,

"You'll regret everything that you have done to me in life" and ended the call.

Giselle frantically tried to call him back, but there was no answer. Afraid he was going to leave the country with her sons, she and her sister rushed to his house, but Ashok and her sons weren't there. His mother, Maya Devi, had no idea where her son was and she, too, was unable to get through on his phone. Giselle and her sister visited various parks looking for them but to no avail. Giselle finally went to the police at 3:40 p.m. and reported them missing.

At around 5:00 p.m., a couple reported to the police that they had seen a man collapsed in the driver's seat of a Mercedes at Crow Road, Lennoxtown.

The police arrived to investigate. The first thing that struck the officers was the over whelming smell of petrol. Peering through the driver's window, the officers noted that the man slumped in the seat had large blisters on his face, bare arms, and on the backs of his hands. The officers sent for an ambulance. They then noticed a large knife, with what looked like blood on the blade, propped between the man's legs.

Looking through the back window, the officers saw a boy, Paul, lying across the back seat and another boy, Jay, lying curled on the rear passenger floor. Both boys had stab wounds to their necks. The officers immediately phoned for back-up and in a short space of time murder detectives and forensic scientists were on the scene, and the road was closed off. Paramedics declared the children had been dead for a few hours, and their bodies were taken away for identification. The driver, Ashok Kalyanjee, was still alive and with ambulance sirens blaring was rushed to the hospital.

Detectives noted that the roof of the car had fire damage and lying near the car a Dictaphone was found along with two empty vodka bottles.

Ashok remained in the hospital recovering from his burns until June of 2008. At first, when well enough to be questioned by detectives, he denied murdering his sons, despite the overwhelming evidence.

Jay Ross

While Ashok was recovering in the hospital from burns and smoke inhalation, Giselle had the unenviable task of burying her sons. She requested the funeral director to spike Paul's hair the way he liked it and to place Jay Ross's favourite toy by his head. She had Paul dressed in his beloved Spider-man pajamas and Jay Ross was dressed in his Bob the Builder costume. Her last request of the funeral director was that they lay embracing each other alongside Giselle's recently deceased mother's ashes in a single white coffin.

Paul

ASHOK KALYANJEE

Giselle had two teddy bear black granite headstones made to mark their grave in the cemetery in Riddrie in the Springburn area of Glasgow.

In November of 2008, Ashok Kalyanjee, at the Paisley High Court, before Judge Lord Brailsford, pleaded guilty to two charges of murder. Ashok's defence lawyer told the court that his client pleaded guilty to both charges of stabbing his sons to death, pouring petrol over them, and trying to set them on fire.

After hearing from the defense and prosecution, the Judge deferred sentencing until January of 2009.

On January 20, 2009 at the Paisley High Court Lord Brailsford sentenced Ashok Kalyanjee to spend at least 17 years in jail after he pled guilty to the murder of his two sons, Paul and Jay, on May 3rd, 2008.

On sentencing, Lord Brailsford made the following statement in court,

"Ashok Kalyanjee – you have pled guilty to the murder on May 3rd, 2008 of your two sons, Paul and

Jay, then aged 6 and 2 years. It is clear that this crime was premeditated, planned, and organized. You used deceit and lies to persuade both the children's mother and the children themselves to go out with you that afternoon. You purchased the murder weapon in advance and also acquired petrol in a can, apparently to incinerate both yourself and the victims at the scene of the crime. The victims were defenceless and in your care. No doubt they loved you and assumed you would care for them as a father should. One of the victims witnessed what happened to his brother. I cannot imagine the suffering that child must have endured before his own murder."

He was sentenced to a minimum of twenty-one years.

Ashok showed no emotion when the sentence was pronounced.

After the court hearing, Giselle said of Ashok,

"Hell is too good a place for him."

Since her sons' funeral, she visits her sons'

graves every day.

Since that time, Giselle Ross and June Thompson have collaborated on a book together of their lives and experiences of dealing with the terrible murders of their children on May 3, 2008. They wrote the book, *Beyond All Evil*, in the hope that it will inspire other women to leave abusive husbands.

BRIAN PHILCOX

Brian Philcox, 53, murdered his two children Amy, seven and Owen, three and then committed suicide on Father's Day Sunday, June 15, 2008. All three had died from inhaling exhaust fumes from the Land Rover in which they were found. A pipe had been placed from the exhaust of the Land Rover in through the back window.

Brian Philcox married the children's mother Evelyn McAuliffe –known as Lyn- in 2000. She had left him earlier in the year because of his violent and controlling personality. At the time of the murders, the couple were involved in an acrimonious divorce.

Brian Philcox, a security guard, was a karate expert and chairman of the Federation of English

Karate Organisations.

On Friday afternoon, June 13th, 2008, Brian picked his children up from his estranged wife, Lyn, at the former family home: a single-story, bungalow-type terrace on the Windmill Hill estate in Runcorn, Cheshire. It was arranged that he would return the children home the following evening.

Brian Philcox

On Saturday evening, Brian Philcox sent Lyn a text message saying he was having trouble with the car.

He later phoned and repeatedly apologized to her. According to Lyn,

"He kept saying: 'There's nothing I can do. It is out of my control. I am sorry.'". She thought he was talking about the car.

He sent another text at 10:45 p.m. telling her to get his spare key and enter his house.

Lyn then telephoned the police and her sister Geraldine who went round to the property. Inside, they found an envelope glued to a kitchen work top with the word 'Bitch' written on it. Police were suspicious of it and called in Army bomb squad experts. They later found that the act of removing the envelope was intended to spark an explosion. Another suspect package was received by a "family member" and this also was removed by explosives experts.

The Police immediately launched a major hunt for Brian and the children. Brian's Landover was found at 3:00 p.m. the following day parked on the edge of a hillside road close to Llanrwst, a remote spot in the heart of Snowdonia in North Wales. Brian, clutching his two children's hands, were all found dead in the back of his Land Rover.

An inquest into the deaths was held at the Llandudno Magistrates' Court in front of coroner John Gittins.

Brian Rodgers, a Home Office pathologist, told the inquest that the children's bodies showed no signs of injury or struggle. They would have been deeply asleep before the carbon monoxide fumes killed them as Brian had sedated them with drugs and a chloroform mask.

The inquest also heard from friends how upset Brian Philcox was by the turmoil of the divorce proceedings and custody battle with his estranged wife. Another friend claimed that Brian had said,

"That woman wants everything - my house and my money and my kids- well I'm not going to let her."

DEADLY DADS OF THE UK

Amy and Owen

In summing up, the coroner, John Gittins, told Lyn McAuliffe,

"When Brian Philcox took Amy and Owen from you, he thought they would be lost to you forever - but he failed. The short lives they had were imprinted on your heart, and they will endure with you. They will be part of you every single moment of every single day."

John Gittens recorded a verdict of suicide on Brian Philcox and verdicts of unlawful killings for daughter Amy and son Owen.

After the inquest, in a statement read out by her sister, Geraldine, Lyn McAuliffe said,

"Since Amy and Owen died, my life has been a constant nightmare. I don't feel as if I have been coping - just existing. No day is easy without them. Some people have mentioned that maybe someday I, or we, as a family will forgive Brian. I will never forgive him for taking our beautiful Amy and Owen. He had no right to take their lives. He was an evil man whose attempts to use homemade bombs clearly show that all his acts were that of a cold-blooded, premeditated killer."

Matt O'Connor, from the now disbanded United Kingdom organization Fathers 4 Justice, said,

"This is yet another tragic case that demonstrates how family breakdown is an unfolding National tragedy for families and children."

CHRIS FOSTER

On August 26, 2008, 50-year-old Chris Foster, a self-made millionaire, killed his 49-year-old wife Jill and 15-year-old daughter Kirstie before torching the family's Shropshire mansion and taking his own life.

Chris Foster came from humble beginnings. As a young boy, his father was a door-to-door salesman in Blackpool selling mattresses. The father then moved his wife Enid and two sons Christopher and Andrew to Wolverhampton in Staffordshire where he had a job as a sales director. As Christopher grew up, according to his family, fires always fascinated him. In fact, he accidentally set fire to his younger brother Andrew when they were boys. Chris was older than Andrew by five years. There was a rivalry between the two boys, who were seldom close during their upbringing. The two boys would often physically fight. Andrew found his brother to be forceful, powerful, and overbearing. He later described him as a bully.

Andrew was also to later claim that when he was about 11 and Christopher 15, his brother had told him the facts of life and showed him pornographic magazines of naked women. Shortly afterwards, Andrew claims Chris started to sexually abuse him. This, he said, would happen at least once a week until he was sexually mature and told Chris he wouldn't do what he wanted any more. Christopher was angry, and the brothers drifted further apart.

Christopher's first job was as an apprentice electrician. However, eventually both brothers became salesmen like their father. Christopher was a successful salesman and maintained a decent living, but he was hungry for more. He coveted a big house and a grand lifestyle with all the trappings.

In 1987, Christopher married bubbly, Wolverhampton-born Jillian Doley. Christopher's big break came when he was watching the news of the

Piper Alpha disaster in the North Sea, 120 miles (193km) off the northeast coast of Scotland in 1988. The fire on the oilrig was devastating and lasted for days. The disaster killed 167 men and only 61 men survived. Christopher saw an opportunity to make a great deal of money if he could develop some kind of insulation that could protect the valves on oilrigs from being destroyed by fire.

Chris came up with a prototype he called *UlvaShield,* patented the idea, and formed a Telford-based company, *Ulva Ltd*. However, the oil companies wanted definite proof it worked. The test to prove it worked was expensive, but Chris was so sure his product was sound that he took a huge risk and mortgaged his smart, modern home in Perton, Wolverhampton to pay for a demonstration.

Enid, his mother, later recalled her son watching the demonstration with his fingers crossed behind his back while the test fire was blazing. She said that Christopher knew that when the fire had died down, if his material had protected the valves, he was made. The test was successful, and the big oil companies wanted it. The Ulva Company quickly became a leading supplier of thermal insulation to oil and gas producers and started to earn huge sums of money.

Chris sold his property in Wolverhampton and moved with his wife to a luxurious country home in the exclusive small Shropshire village of Allscott, near Telford. It was set off a private lane behind gates and had a heated indoor swimming pool. Here, he started mingling in higher social circles and took up country pursuits, such as fishing and shooting. He developed a great passion for guns and shooting and began to build up a collection of expensive guns. Christopher and Jill also went on their first of many luxurious holidays.

Christopher also bought various luxury cars. For his wife, he bought a 4x4 with a JILL40 personalized license plate. Chris started to collect classic cars, which soon became a fleet. At various times, he was seen driving an Aston Martin, a Ferrari, various Porsches, a silver Jaguar, a Mercedes, and a Bentley. In

1993, Chris and Jillian had a baby daughter they named Kirstie.

One Thursday in 2004, while Jill was doing the family grocery shopping in a nearby Sainsbury's, she picked up a copy of the *Shropshire Life* magazine. Back home and flicking through the magazine, she saw a property for sale: the Osbaston House in the village of Maesbrook, Shropshire on the Welsh borders.

It was described as being a Georgian house, built over three stories tall. It included three main reception rooms, three bathrooms, five bedrooms, a cellar, an orangery, various outbuildings, and a gravel driveway on 16.7 acres of land. The land consisted of woodland and had access to fishing on the River Morda. She showed it to her husband who, from an early age, had always wanted a grand house. Chris and Jill went to view the property on the following Saturday and bought it that afternoon for £1.15 million ($1,837,000,000) cash, he later boasted to his mother.

They put their Allscott property on the market

and sold it in October of 2004 for £750,000 ($1,198,000) and moved to Maesbrook. Kirstie, now 11, was enrolled in the independent Ellesmere College, about a thirty-minute drive from the house.

Chris and Jill spent over £200,000 ($320,000) furnishing the mansion with antiques, well over £50,000 ($80,000) landscaping the property, and created an artificial lake. For their daughter, who loved horses, they put up stables, made an exercise yard, divided up the fields into riding paddocks, and bought a tractor. Soon the home also became home to five horses, four dogs, ducks, chickens, and Jill's doves.

Maesbrook is a picture postcard beautiful, affluent village on the Welsh borders. The cars parked in the driveways of the mainly Georgian vine-covered houses were Range Rovers and Porsches. Many of the inhabitants were self-made millionaires from Birmingham and Wolverhampton. It was not long before Chris and Jill made many friends in the community. They would frequently drink with friends and neighbors at the local pub 'The Black Horse Inn.'

DEADLY DADS OF THE UK

Chris Foster was seen as a loving husband and a devoted father. Neighbors remember him as always happy, laughing, and cuddling his bubbly wife Jill and how he 'doted' on his 'horse-mad' daughter Kirstie, who he fully supported and encouraged in her horse jumping. The horses became part of Jill's life, too. Jill treated all the animals like pets, even the chickens had names.

Kirstie Foster

Christopher continued with his hobby he had begun in Allscott of clay pigeon shooting and became a member of the local gun club. Guns and shooting had become central to his life as a country gentleman. He ordered custom-made shotguns from Beretta and Purdey that would cost anywhere from £35,000 ($55,904) to £80,000 ($127,763). It was an expensive hobby, and a three day shoot could cost £8,000 ($12,775.)

Chris had guns all around the house and sometimes he would shoot Jill's doves if they escaped into the garage and deposited droppings on his prized cars. One day, a neighboring farmer complained about Kirstie's black pet Labrador which had been bothering his sheep. Chris got his gun and, much to Jill's and Kirstie's distress, shot the dog. Jill complained to a friend that he was a control freak that had to be totally in control of things.

Apart from the mansion, cars, and gun collections, Chris also apparently had at least eight mistresses on the side. Jill's sister, Anne Giddings, later told the *Sunday People Newspaper* that,

"Jill knew all about his affairs. There were many women on the scene, but she played the dutiful wife and kept quiet. He wasn't a good-looking guy, but money did the talking. He was always flashing the cash - it seemed to give him confidence."

While Chris's insulation invention was a good moneymaker, it wasn't making him enough to support his lavish lifestyle. Christopher was living on credit. In 2003, Christopher Foster's company, Ulva Ltd, had entered into a long-term supply agreement with Cambridgeshire-based DRC Distribution Ltd. to manufacture his invention exclusively. In 2004, Christopher was worth £10m ($15,768,000). However, because of his lavish lifestyle, by 2005, his spending was outstripping his income. Christopher searched and found a cheaper supplier for his invention in California. This was a breach of his contract with DRC Distribution Ltd. who took the case to court. In July of 2007, the case was heard in the High Court and DRC won. In his summation, the judge suggested that "morally" Ulva was in the wrong, leaving DRC out of pocket but in a position to claim back damages, which was believed to be around £800,000 ($1,277,913).

However, throughout 2007, Christopher Foster was making moves to protect his company and its assets. He set up a phoenix company, Ulva Holdings, and by early June of 2007 had transferred most of Ulva's business, its raw materials, goods, plant, equipment, customers, employees, and intellectual property to his new holding company of which he was the director or to himself.

As Christopher Foster's fears and business worries grew, he installed high electric gates, alarms, and CCTV cameras at his home and gave instructions to his housekeeper Belinda Fathers to refuse entry to anyone who was not known to him. He also became paranoid that people were out to get him and began to keep a handgun in his car.

On June 29, Ulva ceased trading and when HM

Revenue & Customs threatened to shut down the company, Christopher Foster brought in administrators, preventing any large claims for damages from DRC Distribution Ltd. as Ulva Ltd had already been stripped of its assets. DRC Distribution Ltd. then applied to the court to have the administrators of Ulva Ltd removed as they alleged they had acted as "stooges" for Mr. Foster and had allowed Mr. Foster to transfer Ulva Ltd's business and assets.

The Court of Appeals agreed. Lord Justice Rimmer said it was "an asset stripping exercise directed at enabling Mr. Foster to carry on his business through another company with a similar name." He added that Mr. Foster was: "...bereft of the basic instincts of commercial morality. He was not to be trusted."

Christopher ended up losing his company and the patent to his invention. He no longer had any salary and a £3m ($4,908,000) freezing order was put on his assets. Added to this, he owed the tax man nearly a million pounds ($1,571,300) as Christopher had resented paying tax. The Inland Revenue had caught up with him. He had earlier bragged to friends that thanks to his 'brilliant accountant' he'd moved so much money offshore that he didn't have to pay taxes like ordinary people.

Christopher, to cut down on his living expenses, no longer visited his shooting club. His local friends and neighbors knew none of his problems. Nor did it appear did his family. Around about August the 20th, the housekeeper arriving for work found attached to the gates a letter which was marked 'to be opened only by Christopher Foster.' She handed it to Chris as he drove out of the gate. It was from the bailiffs. They were going to repossess the house the following week.

Outwardly, Chris appeared as happy and friendly as ever. A few neighbors noticed that he was spending a lot more time at home but the reality was 50-year-old Christopher was not a happy man. He suddenly found he had nothing to do but stay home and look after the mansion and the 15 acres. He busied himself fixing or cleaning something. His paddocks and lake were perfect and his barn was spotless.

THE END

Monday, August 25th, 2008 was an August Bank Holiday. Christopher and Jill and their daughter Kirstie attended their millionaire luxury car dealer neighbor John Hughes' clay shooting party and barbecue. They all appeared happy and in fine form. To his friends and neighbors, he pretended that he was still in business and spoke about an £11million Russian deal that he said was in the pipeline.

The family stayed at the party until well after dark before bidding their farewells. A friend later said,

"They were among the last to leave at around 8:30p.m. and seemed completely normal."

Early in the hours of August 26th, 2008, a 911 call reported a fire at the Osbaston House in the village of Maesbrook, Shropshire. Fire engine crews and police rushed to the scene, arriving at 4:29a.m., where the scale of the fire took everyone by surprise.

When the West Mercia Police attempted to enter the property, they found their way blocked by a horse trailer parked across the gates with its tires shot out and ignition key removed. By the time the horse trailer was removed allowing access to the property, there was little they could do but contain the scene. The intensity of the flames and heat prevented entrance. It took twelve fire crews and three days to contain the flames.

Last photo of the Foster Family

Frustrated, police stood watching for three days as vital evidence went up in smoke. Detective

Superintendent Jon Groves who was leading the investigation said,

"It was like a clay oven turning everything to ash."

As they stood there, they did notice gun cartridges lying around the grounds.

Meanwhile, concerned friends and neighbors, along with the police and firefighters, worried about the Foster family. No one knew if the family was in the blazing mansion. Christopher Foster's mother, Enid, told the police that the last time she had seen the family was at her granddaughter Kirstie's 15th birthday party. As she had left in her car, her son Chris had waved her off saying,

"Bye Mum, see you."

Kirstie's headteacher Brendan Wignall at Ellesmere College said,

"We are very concerned for the safety of Kirstie and her family who are in our thoughts and prayers. Kirstie is a charming, popular, and hard-working girl with many friends, all of whom are hoping that she and her family will be found safe and well."

As the fire blazed, rumors began about the possible cause of the fire. Suspects ranged from disgruntled business associates to the Russian mafia.

Leo Dennis, 42, who was cleared of blackmailing Mr. Foster in 2006, said he believed Mr. Foster had gone on the run because of business problems. He said,

"I don't think he's dead. He's got places he can go, places scattered around Europe. These are properties nobody knows about. In my view, they won't find him when they go in there."

Mr. Dennis added:

"He was not a very nice man and now, with what's happened, it will all come to light, as will everything he was involved in."

Accountant Terence Baines, a former director of Ulva Ltd, said he feared the millionaire may have "just flipped because the pressure of it was too much for him."

Four days later, with the ruins still smoldering and despite the risk of falling debris, investigators entered the house. After three days of searching through the debris, the bodies of Christopher, Jill, and Kirstie Foster were found. After painful research, the police, fire investigators, and forensic team along with footage obtained from the CCTV cameras managed to piece together what they believed happened on that fateful night.

They believe that Jill retired to bed first. From phone records, they found that Kirstie was chatting with a friend online until Chris Foster turned the internet off. Soon after, Kirstie went to sleep. The investigators believed that Chris shot his wife in the back of the head first while she was asleep in bed before crossing the hallway to Kirstie's bedroom, where he shot his fifteen-year-old daughter in the back of the head. He then, it is believed, jammed the horse trailer against the house gates, shooting the tires and removing the ignition keys to prevent anyone from entering the house and intervening.

Chris Foster's last moments were captured by his CCTV cameras. They showed him as a man who was 'calm, collected, and rational.' It shows him at 3:10a.m., approaching the kennels and stable block with a .22 rifle with a silencer and a lamp attached to illuminate his targets. He then shot and killed the family's beloved dogs and horses. Like his wife and daughter, he shot all the animals in the head. He then set fire to the stables and kennels before setting fire to his home, using 200 gallons of oil. He spread oil-soaked rags throughout the house to ensure the fire took hold. Chris Foster, who had made his fortune out of preventing fires, now created one that he hoped would wipe out all traces of his existence.

As the fire took hold, for the last time, he climbed the stairs to his bedroom carrying a loaded gun and lay down beside his murdered wife. He did not shoot himself. Instead, smoke inhalation killed him. A forensics officer commented,

"He shot the dogs in the head, shot the horses in the head, shot the wife in the head. No distinction is there? It indicates he classes them all the same."

As the police were still sifting through the debris of the mansion, the bailiffs arrived. Christopher Foster had dreaded their arrival. Therefore, he left them nothing to collect.

The Foster family was laid to rest on December 19th, 2008. The relatives decided to hold separate funerals. The first was for Kirstie and Jill. A few hours later, Christopher Foster was buried.

INQUEST

In April of 2009, John Ellery, the mid and north Shropshire coroner, held an inquest at Shrewsbury Magistrates' Court into the deaths of Christopher, Jill, and Kirstie Foster. The inquest heard from family, friends, the family doctor, and business associates. It also was shown footage from the CCTV cameras.

The family doctor revealed that Christopher Foster had visited him three times over the last year of his life expressing suicidal thoughts. He put him on anti-depressants in March of 2008.

Mark Bassett, a business associate, told the court that Christopher had confided in him that he'd rather take his own life than lose his family home. He says Chris said:

"…They're not having my stuff. I will top myself. They will carry me out of the house in a box."

Detective Sergeant Jon Groves said,

"He talked to his former associates about using a gun to shoot himself but with the plea of, 'can you look after my wife and daughter?'"

However, they thought he was joking. In addition, during the investigation the police found that on the Friday before he killed himself and his family, he went online and visited a suicide website.

In August, a former partner, Pete Grkinic,

texted Chris asking if he was OK. The reply was,

"Not really. I think everything's coming to a head for me."

The Foster's housekeeper recalled that the last day she worked at the house on Friday August 23rd everything seemed normal with Chris and his family 'larking about'. However, she remembered Chris and Jill had been looking at family photographs, including his childhood pictures. Moreover, they watched their wedding video and cried. She said that,

"Chris had turned 50, so that might have been the reason, but it did cross my mind later that it was a bit strange. Maybe that was part of ending it - a final look at everybody."

A builder friend of Chris's, Gordon Richards, said,

"When I saw Chris a few days ago, he seemed happy, but he said he was feeling the pinch at work because of the credit crunch."

The inquest heard that Chris Foster had been

drinking before the murders and it also heard that he was suffering from a heart defect probably brought on by stress.

The court heard details of his financial situation, how he had the liquidator, the bank, and the Inland Revenue on his back, the bailiffs about to descend, and he'd lost his company. By the end, Christopher owed £2 million ($3,195,127.21) and had remortgaged his home three times. He faced personal ruin.

At the end of the inquest, the coroner, John Ellery, ruled that Christopher Foster unlawfully killed his wife and daughter before committing suicide. He said,

"It's become apparent that Christopher had been mentally ill for some time and had discussed with his general practitioner and other people that he intended to take his own life."

The coroner said Mr. Foster had died as a result of smoke inhalation. Whether or not he intended to turn the loaded rifle recovered from near his body on himself will remain a mystery. The coroner also suggested that perhaps Mr. Foster left the CCTV running as a witness of his actions for those remaining.

Recording his verdict, coroner John Ellery said Mrs. Foster and her daughter had "everything to live for, and Kirstie had her teenage and adult life ahead of her."

After the verdict, Chris Foster's mother Enid said,

"I can't condone what he's done, but I've lost a dearly-loved son, daughter-in-law, and beautiful granddaughter. He talked to nobody. We knew nothing about his financial situation, and it's come as a tremendous shock. They were a very close, loving family unit, and I don't think he could face telling them they were going to lose everything. However, I am in no way condoning what he's done. It's very hard."

Andrew Foster, Chris Foster's younger brother, and Jill's sister Anne were dismayed that even if he felt suicidal, why did he have to take his wife and daughter with him in what seemed like an act of defiance against those coming to destroy their idol?

Andrew commented further,

"They were treated as possessions. It was calculated, premeditated, but it has achieved nothing apart from taking their lives."

Forensics officer Dominic Black said,

> *"I think that Chris Foster did was the most despicable thing I've ever had to deal with. As a father, he had been put on this planet to protect that girl. She was in her own home, in her own bedroom, with her own parents. The safest plae in the world for anybody and he takes her life. That fills me with horror."*

The site where the Foster family house stood has now been cleared.

In 2012, the property went up for sale. It had planning permission for another luxury three-story mansion to be built.

> *"When men are very much in that mode of feeling....their life has been successful....if something threatens to remove all that.....then for some men that loss of power and control will lead to them expressing themselves in this extreme form of violence....it's perverse but it seems a way of regaining some form of control....it's like saying if I can't have all of this, if I can't have my beloved wife and*

child and if I can't have my business and my beautiful home then no one else is going to have them."

Dr. Marilyn Gregor, Researcher of suicide after homicide

DAVID CASS

In September of 2008, car mechanic David Cass, age 33, who was separated from his partner Kerrie Hughes, age 20, suffocated to death their two daughters Isobel, age one, and Ellie, age three. He then rang Kerrie and told her:

"The babies have gone to sleep forever."

He also told her he was going to kill himself.

Kerrie immediately phoned the police and reported the phone call.

Police raced to the caravan in which David lived which was parked on the grounds of the Paynes Road garage where he worked. The police forcibly opened the doors to the garage at around 6:50 p.m. and found David hanged and the two little girls dead in the caravan.

Kerrie, David and Ellie

John Mayhew, the owner of the garage, said that David had worked at the garage on Saturday until 1:00 p.m. David had told his boss John Mayhew that he was depressed about the battle with his ex-girlfriend over the custody of their children.

John Mayhew said of David Cass,

"He was a nice lad, and it sounds ridiculous, but

he was a doting dad. I'd never have thought in a million years he'd harm his children."

That fateful weekend was the first time David Cass had custody of his daughters since his acrimonious split with Kerrie Hughes. He picked up Isobel and Ellie from their mother after finishing work on that Saturday and promised to return them by 7:00 p.m. on Sunday.

Instead, just half an hour before the girls were due back, David made his phone call to Kerrie to say he had killed them.

Ellie & Isobel Cass

A coroner's court issued a verdict of unlawful killing and suicide.

HUGH McFALL

Hugh McFall murdered his wife Susan, 56, and his 18-year-old daughter Francesca at their home in Hampton Road Oswestry, Shropshire, on February 5, 2010.

Hugh & Susan

He first bludgeoned to death his wife of 20 years with one fatal blow to the head as she lay in their marital bed. He then went to his daughter's room and struck her head five times before dragging her, while still alive, and placed her on the bed next to her mother. He left a note next to Francesca which read,

"I love you more than anything I have ever loved. I could not let you suffer, Daddy."

He then rang the emergency services and said,

"Please get to my house. I have killed my wife and daughter. I love them so much."

Susan, Francesca & Hugh

Hugh then left the house and made his way to

premises that he rented for his wholesale flower business in the nearby town of St. Martins. Here, he hanged himself. A suicide note was found next to him in which amongst other things he said,

"It's all over now. I hope I rot in hell."

The day before the massacre, Hugh had learned during a company meeting with his main customer, Stan's Superstore in Oswestry, which supplied him with 95% of his business was suspending further dealings with him amid allegations of invoice discrepancies.

At Shrewsbury Magistrates Court in an inquest into the deaths, the court heard how Hugh McFall faced financial ruin, and a police investigation after his main customer had suspended business with him.

Friends of Mr. McFall related to the court that Hugh had deeply condemned and had been disgusted by the dreadful massacre committed by Christopher Foster who, in August of 2008, had killed his wife and daughter and later himself at Osbaston House in Maesbrook. He was reported as having said,

"How could you do that? How can it get so bad that you could do that to your family?"

Coroner John Ellery, after a two day hearing, in his summing up told the court,

"His financial world had collapsed. His source of business income, or at least 90-95 per cent of it, had disappeared in a moment."

He recorded verdicts of unlawful killing in relation to Susan and Francesca McFall and suicide for Hugh McFall.

WAYNE ACOTT

A 4-month-old baby boy, Mackenzie Acott, died in King's College Hospital in London on January 28, 2011. A post mortem examination found that Mackenzie had suffered a significant traumatic event such as an impact or impacts to his head or a shaking injury.

On the morning of January 21, 2011, at 4:30 a.m., unemployed, twenty-two-year-old Wayne Acott stumbled into his apartment in Sunningdale Court in Square Hill Road, Maidstone. He had been visiting a friend where they had been playing computer games and smoking marijuana. After watching some television, he fell asleep on the sofa at 6:30 a.m.

Susan York, age 30, was Wayne's partner and mother of his son, Mackenzie. A couple of hours later, at 8:45 a.m., Susan attempted to wake him so that he could watch and feed their son, Mackenzie, while she drove her 10-year-old daughter to school. Wayne mumbled and assured her he'd watch him. Susan left Mackenzie in his highchair, happy and contented, and drove her daughter to school.

Susan returned home about 30 minutes later at 9:17 a.m. As she was parking her car, her cell phone rang. It was Wayne panicking and saying he didn't know what was wrong, but the baby had collapsed. Susan ran to their apartment and found Wayne holding baby Mackenzie. The baby's head was floppy, and he was gasping for air.

Susan immediately telephoned for an ambulance and was told to perform CPR on Mackenzie as he had stopped breathing.

When the ambulance arrived, medic Charlene Carter was met by Wayne Acott at the door of the apartment. Wayne told her he had been trying to feed his son when he just stopped breathing. When Charlene entered the apartment, the baby was lying motionless on the floor and was blue. His frantic mother was by his side, attempting CPR.

Charlene immediately began trying to resuscitate the baby boy. Other paramedics arrived and continued the resuscitation efforts. The baby was unresponsive and was unable to breathe on his own.

Mackenzie was taken in very critical condition to Maidstone hospital and was later transported to a special baby care unit at Kings College Hospital in London and put on life support. Baby Mackenzie remained on life support for seven days but died from a trauma suffered to his head after failing to regain consciousness.

The doctors at the hospital were suspicious of abuse, and the police were informed of the incident. Later that morning, they paid a visit to the Sunningdale Court apartment. Here, Police Constable Joanne Hazelwood interviewed Wayne Acott as to the events of the morning.

PC Hazelwood thought that Wayne, whose eyes were red, bleary, and sunken, looked like someone who had been up all night. She found him very lethargic, and his answers were mumbled. He told the PC the same story he had given the medic: that he had attempted to give the baby a bottle and then the baby had developed trouble breathing.

Doctors at the hospital told the baby's mother, Susan York, that Mackenzie's injuries were like those normally seen in victims of a high-speed car accident.

On August 9, 2011, Wayne Acott was charged with the manslaughter of his son. He pled not guilty.

The case was heard in front of a jury in July of 2012 at Maidstone Crown Court in front of Judge Jeremy Carey.

The prosecutor, Sally Howes, alleged that Wayne Acott had, in a moment of frustration and hostility, killed his son. She told the jury that Wayne was unemployed and had recently been fired by his father because he couldn't be bothered to show up for work in the morning. Furthermore, on the night before the assault on his son, he had spent the night watching television and playing on a computer at a neighbor's flat.

He'd returned home at about 4:30a.m. and fell asleep in the living room at about 6:30am on a sofa. In the morning, Susan York, his partner since 2009 and mother of his son, left the flat to take her daughter to school.

Before leaving, she put Mackenzie in his highchair and made attempts to wake Acott up. When Susan left the apartment, the baby was happy and smiling, said Miss Howes.

Miss Howes also told the jury about Wayne's marijuana use, which she said caused conflict between him and Susan York. She said the marijuana affected his sleep pattern, causing him not to go to bed at reasonable times.

Shortly after Susan left, Miss Howes alleged the baby began to cry for his breakfast. She suggested that

Wayne, bleary eyed, bad-tempered, and irritable at having been woken from his sleep had either shaken or thrown Mackenzie so severely onto a soft surface such as a sofa or cushion that he had bleeding to the eye, bleeding to the brain, and brain damage caused by lack of blood flow.

Doctors from London's King's College Hospital told the court that the baby's injuries were so severe they would normally be associated with a high-speed car crash.

A consultant from the hospital, Dr. Tashar Vince, told the court that there was "no naturally occurring process" to cause the injuries. She said the injuries could only be caused by "excessive, unusual force."

When Wayne's defense attorney, Orlando Pownall, called him to the witness stand to give evidence Wayne told the court,

"The second I heard Mackenzie crying, I was awake. I picked him up and put him on my lap. I picked up his bottle. He started struggling to breathe. He was all limp and his breathing was funny," said Wayne Acott.

"I put him on the sofa and called my other half."

Asked by his attorney if he was angry, Wayne replied that, no, he wasn't pissed off.

He told the court that he'd had trouble sleeping because he had been suffering from a toothache and a headache.

When questioned about his marijuana use he said the marijuana didn't affect him at all and that he hadn't even been under the influence of the drug when he woke up that morning.

Susan York testified that her son seemed fine when she left him with his father to take her daughter to school but when she returned, he was gasping for breath and his eyes were fixed.

Wayne Acott was a "good parent" and a "loving father" and on the morning in question he did indeed have a bad toothache. She also said that she didn't believe he'd been using marijuana on the morning Mackenzie collapsed.

When asked by defense attorney, Orlando Pownall, if Mr. Acott had been a good and loving parent, Susan York replied,

"Yes".

Mr. Pownall also asked Susan,

"He perhaps didn't do as much as he could, but he did sometimes help?"

Ms. York replied,

"Yes."

The prosecutor, in closing arguments, said,

"No one will ever know what happened on that fateful day. What we do know is that Mackenzie suffered a sudden and catastrophic collapse caused by trauma to his head, which ultimately led to his tragic death."

On July 25, 2012, the jury found Wayne Acott

guilty of the manslaughter of his son Acott.

Judge Jeremy Carey said the verdict proved Wayne Acott was responsible for the "tragic and wholly avoidable death" of little Mackenzie.

"You were indeed asleep when Mackenzie was crying and crying loudly near you, having been left by his mother in your care. You had been asleep for more than three hours having been up most of the night. You were unhappy about being awoken and, particularly, in those circumstances you had a chronic toothache."

"You had been taking drugs," the judge continued. "I doubt that had any effect on your state of mind at 9 a.m., but that is the backdrop to this offending."

"When Mackenzie did not take his feed, you snapped. It was momentary, but it was devastating in its circumstances because you shook that little baby."

Wayne Acott then shouted at the judge,

"I didn't do anything!"

Judge Carey ignored the outburst and continued,

"You threw him down and caused him appalling injuries about which this jury has heard. I am quite satisfied you had no intention of harming the child and what you did was an expression of your temper. That is the basis on which I will sentence."

"There was here a loss of life and that must be reflected in the sentence. I take into account that not only are you still young, but you are immature."

"You leave behind the inevitable trauma for a mother who has lost a child. I have no doubt the appropriate authority will be concerned about your fitness to be a parent until you reach a level of maturity such that you will be able to control your emotions."

In his sentencing, Judge Carey took into account a 21-month jail sentence Acott was serving for robbing a pizza delivery boy.

Wayne Acott was sentenced to 5 years in prison.

Susan York will spend a lifetime missing her son Mackenzie, which I feel was trivialized by the court as a "momentarily loss of control."

Susan York described Wayne as a good parent. A good parent, I feel, provides a safe and nurturing environment for his child, a roof over the child's head, and food on the child's plate. He provides opportunities for the child to learn, thrive, and grow. He provides a good role model for the child to emulate. He provides help and guidance so that the child grows into a responsible, caring, independent, and law-abiding adult.

What exactly did Wayne Acott provide?

ARAM AZIZ

An Iraqui asylum seeker, Aram Aziz, 32, was found dead on February 12th, 2011 at Watermead Country Park, Leicestershire. He was found hanging in a bird-watching hut. A note left by his side led them to the home of his partner, Joy Small, 24. When they received no answer to their knocks at the apartment in Leicester, they forced entry.

Inside the apartment, the police discovered the bodies of Joy and her and Aram's two children, three-year-old daughter Chanara and two-year-old son Aubarr.

At a coroner's court inquest into the deaths, it was revealed that there had been a history of domestic violence in Aram's and Joy's relationship. Leicestershire Police had been called to the home on at least eight occasions between 2006 and 2010.

In an incident in 2009, Aram had poured lighter fluid over Joy and tried to set her alight after having beaten her. After this, Joy threw Aram out of the home. He was convicted of battering and given a harassment order by the police. The police installed a panic button in Joy's home.

Aziz left a message on Joy's phone saying he would kill her and the children and that she could never have another boyfriend.

A friend of Joy's said Aram was an abusive monster and that Joy was so terrified of him that she slept with a hammer under her pillow. She went on to describe that during the time that they were together, Aziz beat her regularly and once threw a mirror at their son.

At Leicester Coroner's Court, it was ruled that Aram had committed suicide. Unlawful killings by Aram Aziz were recorded for Joy Small, Aubarr, and Chanara.

CERI FULLER

On the morning of July 16th, 2012 in a countryside recreation area of attractive ancient oak woodland with substantial colonies of orchids and long disused quarry workings enhanced by tremendous views across Pontesbury and the Rea Valley in Shropshire, England a member of the public spotted a red Land Rover Freelander which had been reported as missing on the news. He called the police who came to investigate and began a search among the muddy, overgrown paths for the missing occupants believed to be a Mr. Ceri Fuller and his three children.

By the edge of a quarry, the police came upon a scene of unimaginable horror. The bodies of three children: Samuel age 12, Rebecca age 8, and 7-year-old

Charlotte Fuller were found. All three children had been stabbed to death. Sam had died from a single deep wound to his neck, Rebecca had died from five stab wounds to her chest, and Charlotte had died from four chest wounds. Samuel and Rebecca also had cuts on their hands, which looked as if they had desperately tried to defend themselves.

Close by the bodies, wedged into a mound of rocks, a 6.5inch (17cm) bloodstained hunting knife was found. There was no immediate sign of their father. The police later found 35-year-old Ceri Fuller's dead, broken body at the bottom of the 60ft quarry drop with a fractured skull.

CERI FULLER

The Shropshire Quarry

It was estimated that the bodies had been there for several days before being found by police. What happened exactly will never be known, but one can imagine that for the children, who most probably went into the forest willingly and unsuspecting for fun with their father, endured unimaginable horrors of the kind nightmares which are made.

Ceri Fuller was born in the summer of 1997, one of three children born to Geraldine and David Fuller in a maternity hospital in the Forest of Dean. His father David was a biochemist. As a child, he attended Whitecross School in Lydney in the forest of Dean. It was here that he first met his future wife Ruth Tocknel, the daughter of artist Ron Tocknell, and his holistic medical wife, Anne.

While Ruth was artistic, Ceri was academic and earned all As in biology, chemistry, physics, and general studies before going on to study cellular and molecular biology at Huddersfield University, Yorkshire. He graduated in 2001.

Ruth, deeply in love with Ceri, went to live with him in Huddersfield while he studied. They immersed themselves in student life, began drinking heavily, and were frequently violent towards one another. It was in Huddersfield that Ruth gave birth to their son Sam. Shortly after the birth, Ceri and Ruth had a violent row, due to his possessive attitude towards her. After Ceri had punched her 'a few times,' she attempted to phone the police but was stopped by doing so as Ceri tried to strangle her with the telephone cord.

Ruth took the baby Sam and returned to live with her parents in Gloucestershire. Eighteen months later, after he graduated, Ceri returned to the Forest of Dean and he and Ruth moved in together in their own home.

Ceri secured a job as a production line supervisor in 2002 with the global business company, Glatfelter which was a company that manufactured paper-based food and drink products, in nearby Lyndey. At the time, two out of every three teabags used in the world was made by the company.

Ceri and Ruth had two more children. In 2003, Rebecca was born and in 2005, Charlotte completed the family. The girls were bridesmaids when Ceri and Ruth finally tied the knot in August of 2009.

"I feel without doubt that I'm utterly his and he's utterly mine," Ruth wrote on an internet blog she ran.

Photographs from their wedding day show Ruth dressed in a white flowing wedding gown with her arms wrapped around her husband and her head resting on his shoulder while he smiled proudly over her head, as their children happily posed with them. When she posted the photo on the internet, Ruth wrote the caption: ""My babes."

Outwardly, Ceri and Ruth appeared to be a happily married couple but in various posts online, Ruth a talented artist, sculptress, and keen belly dancer, panted a different picture which showed a certain dissatisfaction with the marriage. In 2006, she posted,

Happy Wedding Day

"For the longest time my relationship with Ceri was very fragile and sometimes I still find it hard to have faith in our strength as a couple."

In 2006, when her youngest daughter was one year old, she posted an entry entitled "Bored, bored, bored." In this post, she wrote;

"Oh my god, I'm so bored with myself right now.

When I was younger, I never stayed with the same people doing the same things for very long. Relationships and jobs rarely lasted longer than six months, so I was always meeting someone new.

Don't get me wrong, I'm so glad I finally got over my commitment issues, met the love of my life and settled down to have a family, but sometimes I really feel like I want to break free just for a little while and do something wild."

In July of 2011, the family bought a £162,000 ($259,000) cream pebbledash semi-detached home in the village of Milkwall, in the Forest of Dean, a half-hour walk from the small market town of Coleford.

The children appeared as normal happy children who could frequently be heard by neighbors playing in the garden on a trampoline. The two girls attended St John's Church of England primary school in Coleford, while Sam was a pupil at Lakers School, also in Coleford.

Sam, the oldest, was an articulate, intelligent boy, who seemed to have inherited his father's scientific mind. He was also known to be a "tech head" who loved anything to do with video games and gadgets. His aunt, Joanna Ballard, described him as a "cheeky chappy," who was a lot of fun, always had a ready smile, and who proudly filled the role of the "protective older brother."

The two girls, Rebecca and Charlotte, were more like their mother and enjoyed arts and crafts and dressing up. Rebecca, according to her aunt, was a "shy girly girl, who didn't often talk. She'd walk up to you and whisper in your ear if she wanted a drink."

The aunt said Charlotte – known affectionately

as Charlie, "was the opposite. She was confident and a girly girl who loved to dress as a princess, like something out of a Disney movie. She knew she was cute and would use it."

Mrs. Jan Wagstaff, head teacher of St John's Church of England Primary, said,

"Rebecca and Charlotte were absolutely delightful children and a pleasure to have in school."

Ruth's sister Joanna Ballard lived with her husband Nick and their three children six miles away in Yorkley. The two families spent a great deal of time together. Joanna Ballard said,

"We were particularly close with them as a family, and they would all come over and stay here with us for the weekends. They would all pile into one bedroom, our kids and their kids, so there would be six of them in one bedroom. They were all like brothers and sisters together; they were as close as cousins could be."

Also living nearby in Blakeney, a small village

on the eastern edge of the Forest of Dean, were Ceri's mother Geraldine, 64, and his stepfather Geoffrey Petheram. Ruth's parents Anne and Ronald Tocknell also lived nearby on a leafy street in the small town of Lydney that sits on the west bank of the River Severn in Gloucestershire.

Ruth, in the family's new home, felt increasingly bored and frustrated as a housewife and mother and decided to embark on an Open University Humanities course. Ceri was not happy with Ruth's decision partly because he was so possessive. He was also very quiet and rarely instigated conversations while Ruth was more outgoing and flirtatious. Ceri enjoyed being the sole breadwinner and felt insecure by Ruth's need for greater independence. He insisted on driving Ruth to and from her lectures.

One of Ruth's tutor's was twice-married anthropologist, 38-year-old Mark Lindley-Highfield, the son of a Birmingham warehouse foreman. Before beginning his academic career, he had worked as a finance broker. He styled himself as Mark Paul Lindley-

Highfield of Ballumbie Castle. He had bought the ancient Scottish feudal title 'Baron of Cartsburn' for around £50,000 ($79,000) in 2008. Two years later, he sold the title to an Italian genealogist before buying another feudal title, the Lordship of the Manor of Wilmington in Kent.

Ruth developed a "crush" on Mark Lindley-Highfield. She would later describe it as no more than a schoolgirl crush. As Ruth continued with her course, Ceri became more and more jealous and insecure, and Ruth felt increasingly suffocated and frustrated. Unable to stand it any longer, Ruth told Ceri on the night of July 11th, 2012 that she might go away for a bit, that she thought their marriage was over. She also admitted to her husband that she fancied Mark Lindley-Highfield. Earlier that day, she had sent flirtatious messages to Mark, who lived with his second wife in Gloucester. One of the texts she sent to her tutor referred to a mid-life crisis. He replied reminding her of boundaries that existed between a student and tutor.

Ruth also wrote on Facebook that day that she

was having a 'mid-life crisis.' Later she had added,

"Whew, that's my midlife crisis over with then – and only a few completely bonkers things done. Still, very glad of the urge to reach out to people, loved that."Ceri's sister Abigail had 'liked' the comment.

Emotions were at a boiling point as Ceri and Ruth faced the breakdown of their marriage, A work colleague, Steven Harris, later recollected that he had phoned the house on the evening of July 11th. A child had answered and left the phone with the line still open, and he heard an ongoing row between Ceri and Ruth and distinctly heard the words, "We can't live like this."

Early the following morning, Ruth packed a bag, left for her parent's house, and continued to send 'flirty' texts to Mark Lindley-Highfield but also loving messages to her husband. Later that day, Ruth received a phone call from the children's school asking where the kids were. Ruth began to panic. She had no idea where the children were. She returned to the family home with her father and discovered an empty house but when she found her husband's and son's cell phones, she became filled with a terrible sense of foreboding.

Later in the day, she was seen by a neighbor outside the family's home in a distraught state looking worried and anxious and pacing up and down. The neighbor said,

"At first, I thought she was one of the village drunks but then I recognized her. I thought she might be waiting for someone."

Unable to stand the torment of not knowing where her children were, distraught Ruth swallowed a bunch of pills and attempted to kill herself with a kitchen knife but was prevented by doing so by her father. Her father called emergency services for assistance and telephoned his wife Anne and asked her to join him at the house "as they had a big problem." Ruth Fuller was hospitalized in the Gloucester Royal Infirmary.

While Ruth suspected something terrible was

happening to her three children, the rest of her family believed the children were somewhere safe with Ceri, who had just taken a few days' break. However, given the terrible state his daughter was in, Ron Tocknell contacted the police and reported his son-in-law and grandchildren as missing.

That night, Ruth's sister Joanna sat by her bedside. Joanna found her sister to be in a "zoned out, edgy, and anxious state." She later recalled that Ruth had woken from her tranquilized state late on the night of July 12th and staring into her sister's eyes told her,

"I think that Ceri has killed Rebecca."

The following day, the Gloucestershire Police appealed to the public for sightings of the family and gave a description of the family car. They also issued an urgent appeal for Mr. Fuller to come forward. They described Mr. Fuller's disappearance as 'completely out of character' and stated that the family had no plans to go away.

As Saturday July the 14th came with still no

news, Ron Tocknell posted on his Facebook page,

"If anyone who knows Ceri has any idea of his whereabouts, please contact Gloucester Police immediately. We are all so worried."

Ceri's red Land Rover was spotted in the Leominster area of Herefordshire at around midday on Thursday, July 12th, and later in Newtown, Powys at around 3:00 p.m. CCTV picked them up in the Welshpool area just after 3:30 p.m. It is believed that at some point after this, Ceri drove his children to Poles Coppice at Pontesbury Hill near Shrewsbury in Shropshire, where the car was spotted by a member of the public four days after their disappearance from the family home 75 miles away in the Forest of Dean, Gloucestershire.

As news of the murders reached the shocked residents of the community in which the family lived, candles, flowers, soft toys, and tributes were placed outside the family's house. Reverend Alan Wearmouth, based in Coleford, said that during the days immediately after the news there was a "huge sense of numbness."

Ruth Fuller, the mother of the three children murdered, issued a statement through her family saying that no words could describe her loss and that all she asked was to be left alone to grieve.

Her father-in-law, David, issued a second statement on behalf of both sides of the family which said;

> *"Ceri was a gentle, sensitive and intelligent man but also a very private one. He loved his children dearly and they were such a focal point of his life.*
>
> *"His relationship with each one of them was one of gentleness, involvement and attentive nurturing. Sam, Rebecca and Charlie were such charming*

individuals, brought up in an environment of love.

"We cannot begin to imagine what was going through the mind of this gentle man to drive him to such tragic actions.

"We would ask all to respect our privacy at this time while we try to come to terms with this terrible loss."

INQUEST

A two-day inquest at Edinburgh House Wem Coroner's Court Shropshire to establish the cause of death of Ceri Fuller and his three children heard from friends, relatives, and work colleagues of Ceri Fuller.

Friends of Mr. Fuller described him as a reserved family man, mild-mannered, softly spoken, a good listener who rarely instigated conversations, and who went walking in the country with colleagues. A work colleague, Alan Norton, said Ceri had appeared to be his normal self before he failed to attend work for a night shift on July 12th.

"I didn't notice anything different about him from his usual self, and I didn't notice any changes in his behavior or personality."

His father described him as 'very private' but said his son was suffering from feelings of insecurity about his wife Ruth attending college and had insisted on driving her to and from her tutorials.

Ceri's wife Ruth, who was unable to attend the inquest due to her mental health caused by the tragedy, submitted a statement to the court. In it, she detailed her relationship with her husband. She said that she believed he had killed their children in a "hateful, cruel, and horrible" act and described him as "jealous and possessive."

In her statement, she said that after starting a Humanities course at Cheltenham College, 'everything was changing' in their marriage. She continued by saying,

"We both knew something was going wrong in our relationship, and we were both in a very strange mental state and had been for a while. He was very possessive and jealous and didn't seem to like me talking to anyone. I was changing, and I realized he was feeling neglected. He used to insist on driving me to and picking me up from my tutorials. I think it was his way of making sure I came straight home. It was difficult for Ceri to see me becoming more intelligent, happier, and interacting with other people because he was so possessive."

She admitted in her statement that she had developed a "crush" on her University tutor, Mark Lindley-Highfield, and that Ceri didn't like it. They had discussed separating on the evening of July 11th.

"I told Ceri I needed to go away for a bit," she said. "He thought I may have been going through a mid-life crisis."

Ceri then began "behaving negatively" and took off his wedding ring and started to cry. She added that she had removed her wedding ring months before, as it no longer fit her finger. She recalled that when she discovered the children missing,

"My head was completely broken. I didn't know where the children were, and I didn't know what that meant."

Mrs. Fuller's father Ron described the alarming deterioration in his daughter's mental health when she returned to the family home and discovered her husband had left with her children. Johanna Ballard, Ruth Fuller's sister, told the inquest that Ceri Fuller enjoyed being the sole breadwinner of the family and 'seemed uncomfortable with Ruth wanting anything that wasn't being a mom.' She added,

"They were a very loving couple. There had been a violent incident back when they first got together, but it was a long time ago."

Joanna Ballard also told the court that her sister had told her that she had a romantic crush on her tutor Mark Lindley-Highfield, but she saw it as a schoolgirl crush and had no intention of taking it any further and that there was no suggestion they'd had a relationship. She said they didn't talk in depth about it because she didn't think it was very important.

Deputy coroner, Andrew Barkley, asked Joanne if Mr. Fuller had been "unnaturally -possessive." Joanne said,

"In my opinion, yes, it was 'more possessive' than I would be comfortable with in a relationship. He was very possessive, and she could be very flirty and this could cause problems."

The court heard that on July 11th and July 12th, Ruth Fuller sent five text messages to Mr. Lindley-Highfield and had received six back. In a statement to the inquest,

Mr. Lindley-Highfield told of a text message he received from Ruth. He said,

"I received a text from Ruth asking if I wanted to go and get a drink. I then got another apologizing and saying it was meant for someone called Ceri."

He added, "I replied sarcastically that it was a shame and put 'ha' at the end to make sure."

He said that he had also received a text from her referring to a mid-life crisis, prompting him to remind her of the boundaries between a student and tutor.

The Coroner ruled that their father unlawfully killed the children after 34-year-old student Ruth Fuller announced she was leaving the marriage. Ceri Fuller's death was recorded as a suicide. He added that "overwhelming" evidence had driven him to the "inescapable conclusion" that Mr. Fuller had acted alone in attacking his children at the disused quarry.

Following the inquest, Ruth's father, Ron Tocknell, wrote the following open 1,800-word letter to his local paper.

CERI

"Perhaps some of you feel anger toward him. You know him only as the man who did this.

I know him as the man who fell in love with my daughter. I know him as the man who worked tirelessly to support the family he worshipped.

I know him as the man who, with my daughter, raised my beautiful grandchildren in an environment of love and joy and laughter.

He and Ruth taught them responsibility so they knew why they couldn't always get their own way, and they were able to accept these boundaries with understanding instead of resentment.

I don't think I ever heard the phrase "because I said so" in the Fuller household. When he played with them, it was never as an adult amusing the children. He would surrender himself to the joys of playing as if he, too, were a child.

When he had to address misbehavior, he did so with reason and never with punishment.

Perhaps we will never understand the torment in Ceri's mind that drove him to such an act, but I know this was not an act of malice or spite.

I weep for my daughter's pain, I weep for the loss of my grandchildren, and I weep for Ceri's pain and confusion in equal measures.

There are no villains in this dreadful episode. There are only victims. He will always remain the man I am proud to have called my son-in-law ...

We cannot dictate the random paths our lives take. I would ask you all to suspend judgment and find compassion for all."

CONCLUSION

It is practically impossible to conceive how Ruth Fuller will ever manage to come to terms with the annihilation of the family she treasured or what relief those close to her can give as they attempt to comfort her through her grief.

Ruth once wrote in her blog,

"When the kids are all grown up, Ceri and I have promised that we'll pack up a tartan shopping trolley and drag our dodgy hips off into the sunset together."

That dream has long since evaporated, replaced with a daily living nightmare which no mother should ever have to suffer.

GRAHAM ANDERSON

Graham Anderson, 36, was an unemployed removal man. On Saturday September 1, 2012, he murdered his two sons, Jack, 11 and Bryn, three, before hanging himself at his rented apartment in Tidworth, Wiltshire. His landlady discovered the bodies when she entered the apartment to show prospective new tenants around.

He had been in a stormy relationship with their mother, Victoria Jones, 31, for 16 years before she left him earlier in the year. The relationship was punctuated with accusations of infidelity and violence.

In July of 2011, Victoria had left him and went to stay with a friend. Graham went round to the apartment where she was staying and violently assaulted her and her friend whom he suspected of sleeping with her. He was arrested and jailed for six months.

Despite the abuse, Victoria returned to him for a few months when he was released from prison. Then, unable to stand the abuse any longer, she moved out permanently.

On August 26, while the boys were staying with their father, Victoria changed her status on her Facebook page from single to being in a relationship. This is believed to have triggered the murders.

MICHAEL PEDERSON

In the late afternoon of Sunday September 30, 2012, a dog walker noticed a navy Saab 900 SE Convertible parked at the entrance to a quiet bridle path. It was near the small village of Newton Stacey near Andover, Hampshire. It was made up of only a handful of cottages and country homes. As he walked around the car to enter the bridle path, he saw the body of a dead man and nearby he noticed a child's leg poking out from under a bush. He ran a quarter of a mile to a cottage and telephoned the emergency services.

The police arrived at around 6:15p.m. and found the body of Michael Pedersen, 51, lying face down on top of a knife. Close by were the bodies of his two children Ben, 7, and Freya, his six-year-old sister who was dressed in pink patterned leggings and a pink top, lying on their backs with multiple stab wounds. Ben had a kitchen knife sticking 'bolt upright' in his chest.

A post mortem report conducted on the afternoon of Monday, October 1 found that Ben and Freya both had defensive injuries to their hands and forearms, indicating that they had struggled to escape the violent attack. Ben had six stab wounds, while his younger sister had a stab wound in her heart and in a major artery in her arm.

The post mortem report concluded that Michael Pedersen had stabbed himself three times in his chest, piercing his heart, and once in his forearm. No traces of alcohol, anti-depressants, or other drugs were found in his system.

DEADLY DADS OF THE UK

A number of letters addressed to various people, including Mrs. Pedersen and the police, were discovered inside the Saab.

The police concluded that Michael Pederson, after frenziedly stabbing his innocent children to death, killed himself.

A family friend identified the children's bodies at the Royal Hampshire County Hospital on their distraught mother Erica's behalf. Michael Pedersen was identified by his father.

Ben, Freya and Erica

As news of the murders of the two children spread, friends of the family arrived throughout the day to lay flowers at the door of their £310,000 ($495,000) red-bricked terraced home in Ashford, Middlesex, where the two children lived with their mother, Erica, age 43. A school bag lay in the house porch and the curtains were tightly closed.

The children's grandfather, Erica's father, told waiting journalists of the family's devastation. Speaking outside his daughter's house William Clifford, age 67, said,

"We are obviously devastated and what we would ask is that you respect our privacy in this matter. It is extremely distressing and that is all I want to say."

Teachers, parents, and pupils at the Ashford Church of England primary school which the children attended were shocked to hear the news that the children were dead and wept as they fought to come to terms with the deaths.

A close neighbor told a journalist,

"Erica was a wonderful mom, and those kids were just gorgeous. Nobody can believe that this has happened."

Some neighbors described Pedersen as a doting father and a "lovely man" who would always willingly help out if anyone had a problem. Other neighbors said that the police had been called on a number of occasions over arguments between Michael and Erica at the house.

On Facebook, friends of Michel proclaimed their shock, including one who said, "RIP. Very sad day. Loss of a comrade," while another said, "RIP. Seemed so full of himself in July."

The family had lived together at the house in Ashford until Michael Pederson moved out towards the end of August after a violent argument with his wife of ten years. He went to live with his son from his first marriage, David, in nearby Chertsey, Surrey, two weeks before the murders.

MICHAEL PEDERSON

Michael Pederson

Michael Pedersen wrote on his Facebook page on August 31st, a few weeks before the murders,

> *"Worst day of my life. Sadly have split with Erica, I am absolutely distraught .... still love her very much and would give anything to turn the clock back and try to make things different."*

And in another post he wrote:

> *"Question. Why is it that when you ask someone who is hiding something, why they acted as they did they maintain they were 'drunk', yet when something dreadful happens they maintain they weren't and try to assassinate your good name instead?"*

One friend posted him that his "squaddie buddies" would be there for him if he needed help.

Michael Pederson, originally from Chertsey, Surrey, was an ex-army sergeant in the Household Cavalry who had survived an IRA nail bomb attack escaping serious injury in 1982 at the age of 21. His horse, Sefton, survived the blast, despite suffering from more than 30 wounds from the nail bombs including deep shrapnel wounds and a severed artery. Michael Pedersen and Sefton became national celebrities, with appearances on *Blue Peter* and other television programs. Sefton consequently received a Horse of the Year prize. Four soldiers and seven horses were killed in the IRA attack.

In 1983, he married his first wife, Susan Day, with whom he had two children: Laura and David. When Michael left the Army, he started a career as a truck driver and eventually ran his own haulage company called Highroad Logistics in Ashford, Middlesex.

His first marriage ended in divorce and in 2002 he married his second wife, Erica Arundale, a driving instructor from St Austell, Cornwall. Upon the marriage, Erica became a company secretary of Highroad Logistics and the couple had two children together: Ben and Freya.

DEADLY DADS OF THE UK

Michael and his horse Sefton

During the summer of 2012, Michael and Erica's marriage had begun to crumble apart. Michael had long harbored feelings of jealousy and suspicions of adultery towards his wife. As early as 2004, he was given a caution by police for assaulting a man he suspected of having an affair with Erica.

At the children's funeral, their mother, 43, said, "My angels are in heaven now," as the heart-broken mother released a family photograph of her with Ben and Freya, their faces filled with joy.

MICHAEL PEDERSON

In December of 2012, an inquest was held into the deaths of Michael, Ben, and Freya Pederson in front of Coroner Grahame Short in Winchester, Hampshire.

During the hearing, the coroner heard that Michael Pedersen had recently confided in his doctor that he was suffering from post-traumatic stress disorder as a result of his long army career.

On the day of the killings, the court heard that Michael Pedersen, with his estranged wife's consent, had taken the children to visit his father Brian in Andover, Hants, and the family enjoyed an outing to a lake before having lunch together. Michael was supposed to deliver the children back to their mother by 7 p.m. Instead, he drove his Saab convertible to a remote country lane near the village of Newton Stacey where he killed his children before stabbing himself to death.

Erica Pedersen told the court that over the summer their relationship had deteriorated, that Michael was constantly shouting and accusing her of things, and that many of his outbursts were quite nasty. The police had been called to the family home on a number of occasions.

Matters came to a head during a military reunion party of Michael's on August 25th. At the party, according to testimony given by Erica, her husband had accused her of conducting an affair and told her that she was an unfit mother. He then violently punched her which sent her flying, causing her two black eyes, a split lip, and a broken arm and shoulder.

Erica went to visit her family doctor who advised her to report the attack to the police or her children would be put on the at-risk register. Erica duly reported the attack to the police and began divorce proceedings. The police arrested Michael, and he was served an injunction banning him from the family home. Erica told the court that before he moved out of the house he removed two of her kitchen knives. These knifes were later used in the horrifying murders of his children.

A friend of Michael's told the court that just three days before the murders, Michael had complained to him that Erica had told the police that he had hit her and knocked her over. He claimed to the court that Michael then said,

"She will pay for this."

Another woman referred to him as a "bully and a coward." Several witnesses described Michael Pedersen as a controlling and overbearing bully.

Robert Pedersen, Michael's younger brother, told the court that his brother had been upset with his wife and was also 'angry' with the police whom he felt had not listened to him when questioned about the assault on his wife. He also said that his brother "worshipped the ground Ben and Freya walked on."

Michal's father, Brian Pedersen, told the court that in his opinion Michael had been affected far more by the collapse of his marriage than he had been by his experiences in the Army. He said:

'I think the thing that

hurt him more than anything else was when he was told to leave his house and children and to leave Erica, who he loved in his own way.

'I don't think he could bear to live without all those things and for anyone to say that it was what happened in the Army that affected his judgement - that's wrong.' he said.

At the conclusion of the inquest, the Coroner, Grahame Short, ruled that Ben and Freya had been unlawfully killed by their father and that Michael Pedersen had committed suicide. Mr. Short said,

'It seems to me this was a

pre-conceived decision because of the location chosen. It was on a remote spot in the country where you might assume you were unlikely to be seen or discovered,' he said.

'What happened is beyond comprehension. It must have been terrifying for Ben and Freya in particular to have realised what their father intended and then to be attacked in the way they clearly were.'

Sadly, much of the media, which was widespread, focused on Michael Pederson's early career as a sergeant in the Household Cavalry and his experience of an IRA nail bomb rather than on the murder of the two innocent children and the heartbreak of their bereaved mother. At least one headline referred to Michael Pedersen, who was slightly injured in the 1982 blast, as a hero.

JULIAN STEVENSON

Julian Stevenson, an unemployed Englishman living in the French city of Lyon, married Stephanie, a French woman, in 2005. They had two children together, Mathew and Carla, and lived in the St. Priest suburb of Lyon.

In 2010, Stephanie, an accountant's assistant, moved out of the family apartment with the two children after having been viciously beaten by her husband, who was a heavy drinker. A bitter divorce and custody battle followed the separation. Stephanie argued successfully to the court that because of her husband's violence and alcoholism, he should not be allowed unsupervised access with the children.

However, that order was overturned in May of

2013 and the two children Matthew, 10, and Carla, 5, were allowed to spend the first overnight unsupervised visit with their father. Their mother dropped the children off at her ex-husband's apartment early in the evening of Friday May 17th.

On Saturday May 18th, Julian Stevenson, 47, was seen with his children wandering around the neighbourhood of his apartment looking "calm and relaxed while the children were smiling happily." Julian took them for lunch at McDonald's and then to the bakery to buy sweets and little presents before taking them back to his apartment.

At around 5:00 p.m. on Saturday May 18th, Stephanie went to collect Matthew and Carla from their father. She saw Julian looking panicked and angry in the stairwell of the apartment block, with his clothes covered in blood. He ran out of the building and made his way off on a pair of roller-skates.

Panic stricken, Stephanie called the police. When the police arrived, they had to break into the apartment where they found Matthew and Carla dead with their throats slit.

After a short manhunt, Julian was found at around 8:00 p.m. that same evening.

On Monday May 20th, Julian Stevenson appeared in the Tribunal de Grande Instance, Lyon's main criminal court, where the allegations against him were formally read out. He allegedly confessed to killing his two children by slitting their throats but did not give many more details.

A judicial source said the murders were "clearly linked to the marital breakdown and the right of access to the children which the father deemed insufficient."

Julian Stevenson's trial is still pending.

CONCLUSION

As can be seen in the twenty-six profiles contained in this book, the majority of these crimes have been committed due to marital breakdown or male sexual jealousy. Five were committed due to financial concerns and in one case, that of Wayne Accott, by complete irresponsibility and rage.

In the cases due to financial worries, the entire family was killed. The only case that is the exception is the one involving Philip Austin in which he and his wife bickered frequently about money, causing him to lose his temper and then deliberately murder his

CONCLUSION

children. Philip Austin survived and is currently serving a long prison sentence.

But what drives people such as Chris Foster, Robert Mochrie, and Hugh McFall, who are so often described as being devoted to their families, to carry out such a brutal crime? And can anything be done to prevent it?

In the United States, which now sees ten murder-suicides a week, these killers are known as the "family annihilator," and virtually all are premeditated. The director of the Brudnick Centre on Conflict and Violence, Professor Jack Levin, from Northeastern University in Boston says, "The family annihilator is a middle-aged white man, a good father, a good husband, a responsible provider, who suffers a catastrophic loss, usually financial. They become despondent, hopeless about the future, and usually blame everyone else apart from themselves."

Family annihilators normally have no prior criminal record, but they share one key characteristic:

"They are loners," says Jack Levin. "These killers don't share responsibility. They have the mental attitude that they are 'commander-in-chief', and that it's lonely at the top. They cannot share their problems with the foot soldiers." Worried about what will happen to their children and wives after their death, they convince themselves that it would be better to take them with them. Family annihilators go to great lengths to plan their crimes; they do not kill in the heat of the moment, or in a fit of rage. "They are very methodical," says Jack Levin. "They plan it out for a long time.

Chris Foster, Robert Mochrie, and Hugh McFall saw no means of escape, no way of preventing their idyll lifestyles and facades of happy family life, from hurtling to disaster. And it would appear that in their disturbed minds, the only way to turn this around was to destroy the families they loved.

Even as Chris Foster and Robert Mochrie prowled their houses, moving from room to room, killing as they went, it is highly likely that they still thought of themselves as loving dads and husbands

CONCLUSION

protecting their families from the horrors of the world.

Remember Hugh McFall's letter to his daughter. "I love you more than anything I have ever loved. I could not let you suffer, Daddy."

While Christopher Foster's security cameras showed him driving a horsebox to the front gates before shooting the tires to prevent emergency services accessing the property, thus keeping the world at bay. Twisted love?

MARITAL BREAKDOWN

In the twenty profiles of marital breakdown killings, four of the cases, Karl Bluestone, Jaya Chiti, Richard Hicks, and Aram Aziz, resulted in all of the wives been murdered as well as nearly all of the children and the father committing suicide. All the killings were fuelled by jealousy. Except for the case of Jaya Chiti, all of the three other cases had a history of physical abuse by the husband in the marriage. The Director of the Greater London Domestic Violence Project, Davina James-Hanman, says, "Domestic violence, whether sustained or carried out in a single killing, is essentially about power and control."

REVENGE

It is nearly impossible to try and begin to understand the mentality of a father who is willing to murder his own children over an issue of revenge but in many of these cases, it is a clear motive. He feels he has lost control and kills his children to get even with his wife because he hates her and he blames her. He knows that she will suffer for the rest of her life if he murders the children and leaves her alive.

Unfortunately, in some instances, such as in the case of Gavin Hall, who murdered his daughter Millie for revenge, the tabloid press focused on his wife's behaviour as the trigger for the crime. One headline screamed: "The judge, his sordid affair, and the husband driven to murder". While another proclaimed: "Sex obsession of devoted mother blamed for murder of innocent child."

Superintendent John Jones, who led the murder

inquiry, was angered by these press reports that Gavin Hall's wife's infidelity was responsible for the murder of their daughter Millie. He said: "Affairs happen all the time and people don't respond by killing their children." It is more of a case of aggressive revenge – "I'm going to hurt you like you hurt me" mentality. Surely in these cases, the mother should be allowed to grieve in peace without the press putting the blame on her for the father's inhumane behavior.

CUSTODY BATTLES

Many of the marital breakdown cases involved child custody battles. In many cases, the father couldn't accept that the marriage was over and someone else has moved in with his ex-wife and is now the father of his children.

Forensic pathologist, Dr. Chris Milroy, who studies murder-suicides, says that "When men kill their children, there tends to be revenge in the equation. It's like they're saying, 'If I can't have them, no one can.'" As if they are his possessions.

Men who kill their children do so because they choose to; because they believe they own their children. These murders are not accidents but are normally pre-mediated and only extremely rarely are they caused by mental illness.

There are no excuses for killing children. Divorce is not an excuse. An affair is not an excuse. Nor is financial failure.

Is it possible, one wonders, whether such horrific crimes can be prevented? Depressingly, the majority of experts agree that it is a practically impossible task and that a great deal more research needs to be done in these types of murder.

To all the victims and surviving family members of these horrific crimes, one can only feel great sadness.

May all the innocent victims rest in peace.

OTHER BOOKS BY SYLVIA PERRINI

WOMEN SERIAL KILLERS OF THE 17th CENTURY (WOMEN WHO KILL)

ASIN:B00BKPWKG6

ISBN-10: 1482657805

ISBN-13: 978-1482657807

This was the century when royal poison scandals sent shockwaves throughout Europe. The scandals so rocked France, that Louis XIV in 1662, passed a law stopping the sale of poisonous substances to people other than professionals, and for all purchasers to be registered.

In this short booklet of approximately 9,300 words, best selling author Sylvia Perrini takes a look at some of the most prolific women poisoners of this century, and a look at one woman, who did not use poison, just torture.

Be prepared to be shocked.

WOMEN MURDERERS OF THE 18th CENTURY (WOMEN WHO KILL)

ASIN:B007B2G0KY

ISBN-13:978-1482678642

Why do women kill and murder? They are supposed to be the gentler sex, the ones who nurture the babies and support families, keeping the very structure of society in place. Why do some women go wrong? Is it greed, jealousy, power or just plain wickedness?

Women Murderers have been around for centuries. In this short book of approximately 12,500 words best selling author Sylvia Perrini looks at the profiles of eight women who operated in the 18th century.

WOMEN SERIAL KILLERS OF THE 19th CENTURY: THE GOLDEN AGE OF POISONS (WOMEN WHO KILL)

ASIN:B00BK9QY2S

ISBN-13: 978-1482696721

The 19th Century is often regarded as the heyday of poisoners. In the beginning to the middle of the nineteenth century, a poisoning panic engrossed the public imagination. In the Times newspaper in England, between 1830 and 1839, fifty-nine cases of murder by poisoning were reported. By the 1840s, the number reported had risen to hundreds. And, of these hundreds of poisonings, sixty percent involved women murderers.

In this fascinating book, best selling author Sylvia Perrini, looks at serial women killers around the world in the 19th Century. Nearly all the cases, but not all, involve poisoning.

WOMEN SERIAL KILLERS OF THE 20th CENTURY

ASIN:B00C0JRMFA

ISBN-13: 978-1483953960

The 20th-century, like the previous centuries, has seen no end of murders by women with poison as their choice of weapon. Furthermore, just like in the previous centuries, the murders have been just as cold and calculating.

Those lucky few who have managed to survive an attempted murder by these women have described being poisoned as being equal to being devoured alive.

However, the 20th century has also seen murders committed by women with guns and, in the case of Dana Gray, with physical violence. Dana is a rarity among women serial killers, in both her choice of victim and her hands-on method of using her hands, a cord or rope, and an object with which to batter her victim.

Yet, even after all this time, we are left with the

same question: what leads a woman to commit serial murder?

In this book, the author examines the profiles of twenty-five women serial killers, all of whom acted alone.

Ms. Perrini has not included mothers who solely kill their own children as she believes that is a subject that deserves to be written about entirely separately.

Even leaving those specific types of Women Serial Killers aside, there are still many women who choose to commit murder again, and again, and again…

Welcome to the world of 20th century women serial killers.

OR BUY THE ABOVE FOUR BOOKS IN ONE

WOMEN SERIAL KILLERS THROUGH TIME Boxed Set (4 in 1)

ASIN: B00C3N7BFY

ISBN-13: 978-1484044261

I DON'T LIKE MONDAYS: FEMALE RAMPAGE KILLERS (WOMEN WHO KILL)

ASIN: B00CW16O28

ISBN-13: 978-1489533968

The Famous hit song "I don't like Mondays" penned by Bob Geldof, was written after the school shootings in San Diego, California, committed by Brenda Spencer. Once she was apprehended and asked why she had done it. Her reply was:

"I don't like Mondays, do you?"

When one thinks of spree killers or rampage killers, normally one thinks of a male. Men such as the Aurora Colorado Movie Theater James Eagan Holmes, Seung-Hui Cho Virginia Tech Massacre, Columbine school killers Eric David Bennet and Dylan Bennet

Klebold, Adam Lanza at Sandy Hook Elementary School, and the 2011 massacre at a summer camp in Norway, by Anders Behring Breivik to name just a few.

Yet, women have also committed these crimes just not in such large numbers as men

SUGAR N`SPICE: TEEN GIRLS WHO KILL (FEMALE KILLERS)

ASIN: B00DESV62Q

ISBN-13: 978-1490458458

Murder is horrific whenever it happens and in what ever circumstances. But when a murder is carried out by a young girl, not much more than a child, it is doubly horrific.

What is it that goes wrong in the lives and minds of these girls that grow up to be teenage killers? Girls who ruthlessly murder strangers, young children, parents, and others?"

In this short book of approximately 25,000

words Sylvia Perrini has selected seven murder cases committed by teenage girls. The profiles of the girls covered are;

PAULINE PARKER AND JULIET HULME aka Anne Perry, the well-known author of murder fiction.
BRENDA ANN SPENCER
CHERYL PIERSON
HOLLY HARVEY AND SANDRA KETCHUM
CHELSEA O'MAHONEY
CINDY COLLIER AND SHIRLEY WOLF
ALYSSA BUSTAMANTE

BABY FARMERS OF THE 19th CENTURY (WOMEN WHO KILL)

ASIN:B00ACPGTFI

ISBN-13: 978-1484128725

The practice of baby farming came about in late Victorian times. In this era, there was a great social stigma attached to having a child out of marriage and no adequate contraception existed. In this period of time, no child protection services or regulated adoption agencies were in existence.

A number of untrained women offered adoption and fostering services to unmarried mothers who would hand over their baby and a cash payment. The mothers hoped that this payment would find stable, happy homes for their babies. And in the case of weekly payments that they would at some time in the future be able to re-claim their child.

It was, without doubt, one of the most sickening aspects of Victorian times, not only in Britain but also in its colonies as well.

Many of these fostering and adoption agencies were bona fide, but a frightening number were not. They became known as baby farms.

In this short book, best selling author, Sylvia Perrini, introduces us to some of these baby farmers.

NO, DAD! PLEASE, DON'T! (THE JOHN LIST STORY) (MURDER IN THE FAMILY) [Kindle Edition]

ASIN: B00EI2BA28
COMING OUT IN PAPERBACK SOON

On the morning of December the 8th, 1971, New Jersey, and indeed the entire metropolitan New York City area, awoke to lurid newspaper headlines of the horrific massacre of almost an entire family in the affluent community of Westfield, N.J.; a story that both captivated and horrified a nation. The story was quickly picked up around the world.

The face of John List, who had left letters confessing to the crime, stared out at the readers. He was an ordinary, fairly non-descript looking man. The question on everyone's lips as news broke of the horrific slaughter by a college-educated, seemingly successful accountant, and Sunday school teacher was why? He had murdered his mother, wife and three teenage children.

In this short booklet, of approximately 11,000 words, best selling author, Sylvia Perrini, delves into the events that led to the horrific slaughter of John Lists, mother, wife and three teenage children.

John List managed to evade capture for over 18 years and never expressed remorse for his crimes.

Printed in Great Britain
by Amazon